Home and Community Influences on Young Children

Home and Community Influences on Young Children

Karen Dahlberg Vander Ven

DELMAR PUBLISHERS
COPYRIGHT © 1977
BY LITTON EDUCATIONAL PUBLISHING, INC.

All rights reserved. No part of this work covered by the copyright hereon may be reproduced or used in any form or by any means — graphic, electronic, or mechanical, including photocopying, recording, taping, or information storage and retrieval systems — without written permission of the publisher.   10 9 8 7 6 5 4 3

LIBRARY OF CONGRESS CATALOG CARD NUMBER: 76-14092

Printed in the United States of America
Published Simultaneously in Canada by
Delmar Publishers, A Division of
Van Nostrand Reinhold, Ltd.

Jeanne Machado —
Consulting Editor

Elinor Gunnerson —
Early Childhood Education Series Editor

Michael Moody —
Photographer

DELMAR PUBLISHERS • ALBANY, NEW YORK 12205
A DIVISION OF LITTON EDUCATIONAL PUBLISHING, INC.

Preface

"Why study the child outside the classroom?", the prospective teacher may ask. There are several reasons. First of all, there is increasing evidence that those programs which recognize the significant role of the family in promoting the child's development and include parents as well as children within their scope are the most effective. Then, each individual child in a preschool or day care program brings to it his own ways of viewing and relating to the world. He is the product of a unique interaction of biological givens, family relationships, and learning experiences to which he has been exposed. Understanding and working with the influences on the child outside of the classroom setting adds depth and meaning to the teacher's classroom activities.

The significance of a child's earliest experiences for his sound development are widely recognized. *Home and Community Influences on Young Children* describes the ways in which this seems to be so. For many children, it has been found, there are lacks in important early experiences. They may not have close relationships with caretakers and sufficient stimulation or play. They may live in families with insufficient incomes.

Programs have been developed to intervene in, or make up for, such lacks early in the child's life. It is hoped that by the time he begins grade school, he may have been helped to achieve the experiences which are related to later school success. Since the philosophy of many preschool and day care programs is to intervene in the developmental process, this text explores that concept and the way it is actually carried out.

Along with interventive programs, today's changes in society are bringing the care of young children out of the home. This text describes some of the types of programs which are available to families wishing substitute child care. It also discusses some of the issues which must be considered so that such programs have a positive effect on both families and children.

Although some critics have stated that day care and other child care programs do not support the family, this does not have to be so. Careful planning for positive school-home relationships, effective communication, and parent involvement school activities serves to strengthen the family as well as to contribute to the development of the child himself. Parents frequently turn to their children's schools for guidance in the complicated job of parenting. This text introduces the prospective teacher to the many aspects of working with parents.

Increasing recognition is being made of the exceptional child in the community and of meeting his needs. Therefore, the student of normal development should also be attuned to the child with special needs. No longer are these children excluded from programs with other children. Early identification of the exceptional child can help provide him special help so that he is most likely to be able to join his peers when he reaches school entrance age.

Finally, the teacher attuned to the wider, community-based influences on child care should be familiar with the significance of community understanding and acceptance of her program, how to work with the community to achieve it, and, particularly, how to seek the financial support without which there can be no programs.

Through its sectional coverage of these various community-related topics, *Home and Community Influences on Young Children* helps prospective teachers develop a familiarity with the wide variety of related influences on any preschool program and the children within it. This awareness should enrich their understanding of the complex world in which the children with whom they will work are being raised.

Each unit of the text is introduced by behavioral objectives. Answers are provided for the objective type review questions to facilitate individual study and self-evaluation.

Karen VanderVen's educational background is in psychology, child development, and education. She is presently Associate Professor of Child Development and Child Care, School of Health Related Professions, University of Pittsburgh, teaching at both the undergraduate and graduate levels and serving as coordinator of field placements for the Department. From 1973 to 1975 she was Project Director of the National Institute of Mental Health grant in support of the Baccalaureate Program in Child Development and Child Care at the University of Pittsburgh.

Dr. VanderVen has worked with both normal and atypical children and with parents, in a variety of settings. She is joint author of *Child Care Work With Emotionally Disturbed Children,* now in its second printing, and is the author of several other professional publications. Presently, she is a Contributing Editor of *The Child Care Quarterly.*

Preface

Other texts in the Delmar Early Childhood Education Series are

Creative Activities for Young Children — Mayesky, Neuman, and Wlodkowski
Teaching Young Children — Beatrice Martin
Early Childhood Experiences in Language Arts — Jeanne Machado
Administration of Schools for Young Children — Phyllis Click
Early Childhood Development and Education — Jeanne Mack
Experiences in Music for Young Children — M.C. Weller Pugmire
Early Childhood Education in the Home — Elinor Massoglia

To

Genevieve W. Foster   Margaret B. Mc Farland

Contents

SECTION 1 EARLY EXPERIENCE

Unit 1 Factors Influencing Child Development   1
Unit 2 Cultural Influences on Child Rearing Practices 13

SECTION 2 EARLY INTERVENTION

Unit 3 The Concept of Early Intervention 25
Unit 4 Models of Early Intervention Programs 35

SECTION 3 SUBSTITUTE CHILD CARE

Unit 5 Child Care and the Changing Society 44
Unit 6 Special Aspects of Contemporary Child Rearing 51
Unit 7 Models of Substitute Child Care 59

SECTION 4 PARENT-TEACHER CONTACTS

Unit 8 Establishing Parent-Teacher Contacts 68
Unit 9 Parent Involvement 76
Unit 10 Parent Education 84
Unit 11 Working With Parents and Children in the Home 95

SECTION 5 THE EXCEPTIONAL CHILD

Unit 12 Identifying the Exceptional Child 105
Unit 13 The Exceptional Child in Class and Community 113

SECTION 6 COMMUNITY RELATIONSHIPS

Unit 14 Program Resources and the Community 120
Unit 15 Political Factors in Contemporary Child Care 128

Answers to Review 138

Bibliography 140

Index 145

Section 1 Early Experience

unit 1 factors influencing child development

OBJECTIVES

After studying this unit, the student should be able to

- Relate the effects of parent-child interaction to the child's later development.
- Describe the processes of attachment and mutuality and of separation and detachment.
- Define the concepts which help explain the foundations of psychological development.
- Define and describe dimensions of "basic temperament" and their implications for understanding individuality.

The newborn infant does not develop into a human being in a vacuum. From the time he enters the world, both the way others care for him and the physical environment in which he lives exert an influence on his development. At the same time, his own unique characteristics affect the way his environment responds to him.

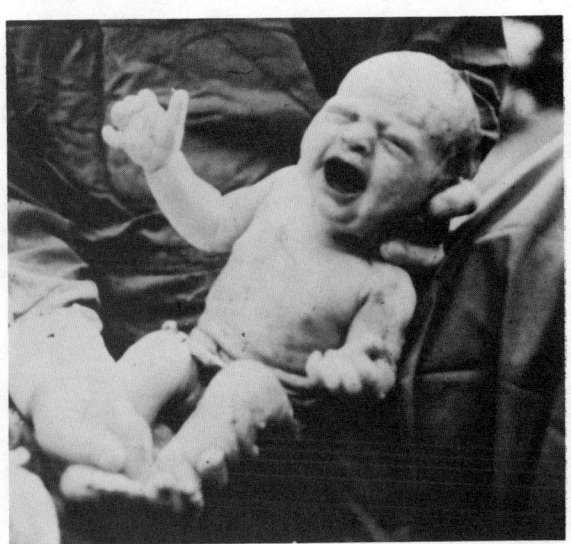

The person working with young children must know about the different kinds of early experiences in infancy which build on genetic factors to provide the foundation for the ongoing psychological and social development of the child. These experiences can help ensure that the child achieves his full potential. Important principles upon which early childhood programs are structured are based on them. The first person outside the home to whom the young child relates is often a staff member of an early childhood center. Therefore, it is crucial that this person recognizes the role of the physical environment and interpersonal experiences on the developing child.

In the study of human behavior over the past hundred years, one of the major concerns has been the identification of the conditions which promote the growth of a child into a mentally healthy adult. As a result, there is agreement that the overall quality of a child's early experience is related to his later intellectual and personality development.

Section 1 Early Experience

THE SIGNIFICANCE OF THE MOTHER-CHILD RELATIONSHIP

It is recognized that, since she is usually the person who is most directly involved in the nurturing of the young infant, the mother must have a substantial influence on the course of the child's development. More recently, it has been recognized that there are other strong influences, too. These include basic temperament, the father, the physical environment, and other caretakers. This unit describes the nature of these early influences.

The Concept of Basic Trust

Descriptions have been made of tasks or outcomes which must be achieved before a child can move sucessfully from one stage of development to the next. Knowledge of them can help those working with children provide the experiences necessary to achieve these goals.

In his well known and respected developmental theory, "The Eight Stages of Man," Erik Erikson describes the major outcome of infancy as the child's experiencing either a feeling of basic trust or mistrust. Achieving trust, the infant comes to feel warm and confident about the world and the people in it. He has an inner sense of the goodness of himself and others. On the other hand, the outcome of infancy may be a sense of mistrust. When this is the case, the infant feels that the world is a frustrating, ungratifying place in which his needs are not met. He does not feel that he is a good person.

Whether the young infant develops a sense of trust or of mistrust depends on the quality of the physical and the psychological care he receives. The infant is completely dependent on his mother and any others taking part in his care for the satisfaction of his basic needs. They provide him with warmth, with food, with overall comfort. How they meet these needs — how they feed him, how and when they respond to his cries of distress, how they hold him when diapering him — all of these add up to the total pattern of care which determines the degree to which basic trust is achieved.

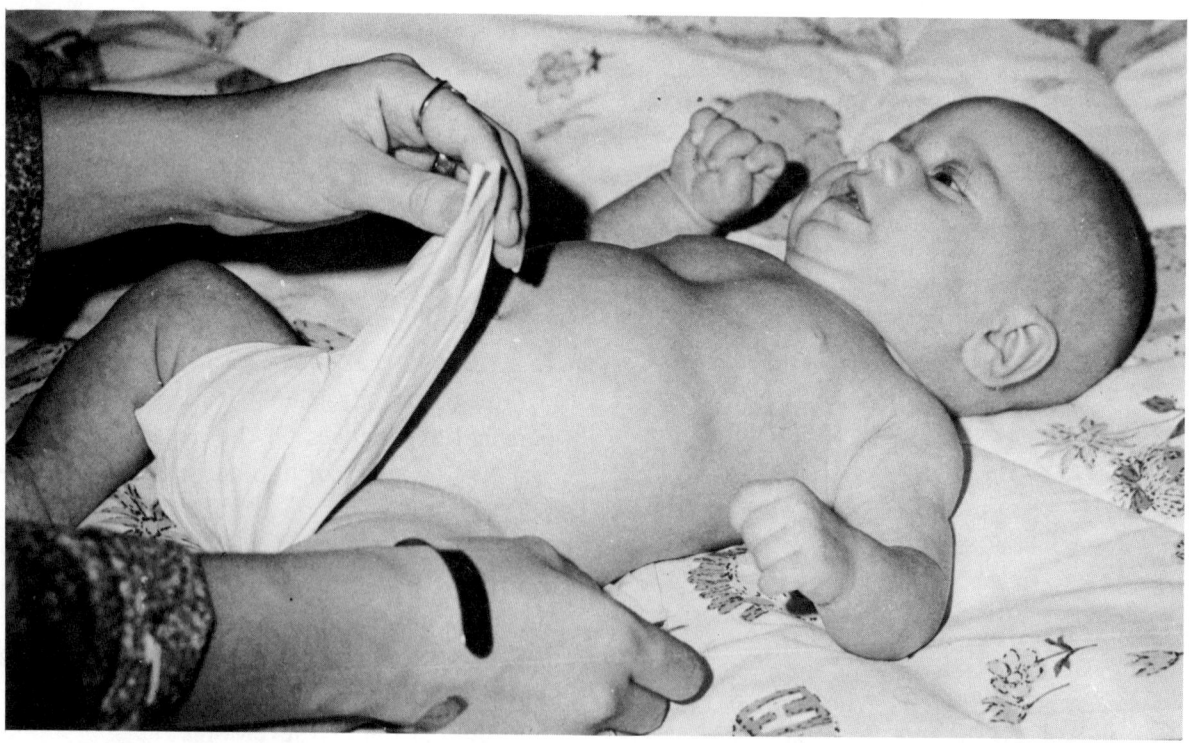

It is the total emotional climate which the child experiences, rather than any particular method or technique of child rearing, that has the major influence on the developmental outcome of a particular stage. There are, however, some basic processes which contribute towards the infant's becoming a human being, and, hopefully, a trusting one. Attachment is one of the most important of these.

The Concept of Attachment

Research on infant-caretaker relationships shows that both human and animal babies exhibit a strong drive to relate to, or become *attached* to, their caretakers. Attachment is not a one-way process, however. The striving of the baby to form a bond with its mother evokes in her a warmth and responsiveness. To mother or nurture an infant does not mean routine care to a passive being.

Rather, the mother and baby are "cued" to each other. There is a mutuality in their relationship. This, in turn, encourages further interaction which continues to cement and develop the attachment process. When, for example, a baby adjusts his body to his mother as she picks him up, her feeling of warmth for him is stimulated. The responsiveness of a baby to his mother — to her voice, to her smile, to the feeling of her body, to the games she plays with him — is gratifying to both. The cues the baby thus gives the mother help her organize his experiences in a way that meets his needs at a particular time. A baby, for example, may enjoy being held in a certain way when he is tired. His mother will position him this way when she knows he has not had much sleep. This mutual feedback between mother and child is a key factor in the development of the baby's sense of basic trust and attachment.

Basic temperament, or individuality, of both mother and child exerts an influence on the particular nature of the attachment bond which develops between the two. Both mother and child need to gradually adjust to the "style" of responding of the other. The adult adapts more readily than the infant.

Touching is an important part of the mother-infant tie. Research by the psychologist Harlow indicates that simply receiving nourishment and being able to nurse are not enough to form a bond of mutual affection between infants and mothers. Rather, it is the opportunity for there to be mutual physical contact during the feeding process which is significant. In fact, Harlow suggests that it may actually be a function of nursing to ensure that the infant has close body contact with its mother. This is perhaps one reason why child development specialists stress the importance of holding infants as they are being bottle fed. The Harlow experiments were done with monkeys. It seems quite likely, however, that his findings are relevant to human beings.

In demonstrating attachment, individual infants respond in different ways to their primary caretakers. Ainsworth, another famous researcher in the area of infant attachment, has described the ways infants show their growing

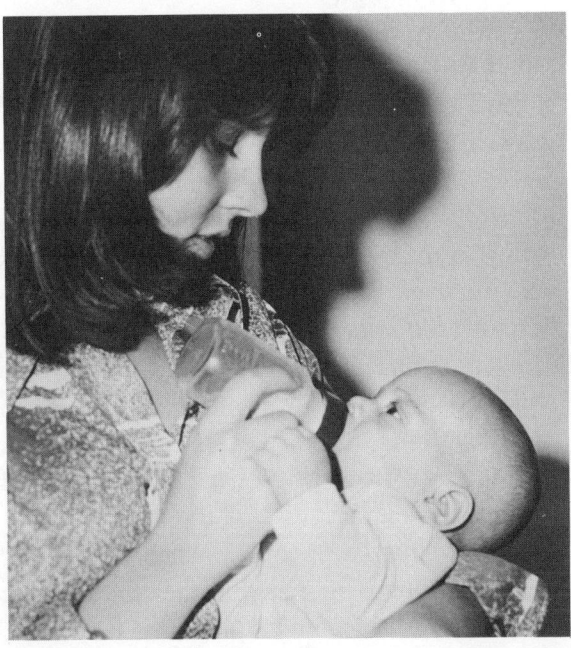

bond with their mothers. They may smile when interacting with them more than with other people. They may follow their mothers' movements with their eyes or physically, when they are able. Older babies may respond to the approach of their mother by lifting their arms, smiling, or other similar responses. Both Harlow and Ainsworth cite the importance of the mother's presence to the child in times of danger or fear-producing situations. At these times, the baby turns to the mother rather than to another available person for protection or solace.

The process of attachment in infants follows a developmental pattern. At the beginning of life, the youngest infant may not show a selective response to his mother. Soon, however, his response becomes more pronounced and intense. Finally, the pattern of exclusive attachment to the mother gives way to one of beginning to form relationships with others as well. The nearness of his mother supports the young child during his first explorations.

MATERNAL DEPRIVATION AND RELATED CONCEPTS

The essential factors of the early mother-child relationship which provide the foundation for sound mental and emotional health in the child have been described. *Maternal deprivation* is a concept which describes the condition in which infants totally lack a close and consistent relationship with a mothering person. It, too, has an important bearing on the planning of substitute care for young children. It also has had an influence on the shaping of attitudes towards mothers and the ways they bring up their children.

Some years ago, children who were being raised in institutions were observed. They did not seem to be developing properly. The pattern of care received by such infants was very different from that experienced by children being raised within the typical family unit. Large groups of children were housed in drab, colorless surroundings with just a few caretakers or attendants. This situation was quite different from that of the single baby housed in a colorful nursery room with his own mother on hand to give him individual care. Feeding, bathing, and changing were done because they were necessary and were done quickly and routinely. It was not possible for busy attendants to respond intimately to each child — to cuddle, look at, and talk to each one.

Since the babies were cared for by different people at different times, no one person could come to understand the particular needs of an individual baby and how they should be met. The babies' beginning attempts to explore the world and other people were not met with an encouraging adult response.

Except for the times they were briefly removed to receive basic physical care, the babies were left in their cribs. They had no chance to observe the hustle and bustle of adult activity. They could not develop their physical skills and awareness of the environment by crawling on the floor. There were few, if any, toys or colorful objects in the babies' living area.

The babies raised in these environments failed to develop normally. Some even died. They became increasingly *apathetic* (withdrawn) and listless in their drab and loveless world. They seemed not to have the strength to ward off illness or to hold an interest in the world to make them want to live. The babies who survived did not behave or continue to develop the way normal babies do. They showed strange, repetitive behavior. Some rocked back and forth, continuously trying to provide from within the stimulation which was lacking from without. Others banged their heads on the sides of their cribs. They did not respond to people. When picked up, the babies just lay limply rather than fitting their bodies to accommodate their caretaker.

They did not smile or make eye contact. It appeared that the learning ability of these babies was severely impaired. They were not developing physically or emotionally and were not having their curiosity stimulated by exposure to different experiences. Therefore, their ability to *learn,* to develop new and more complex behavior, was severely impaired.

When the devastating effects on these infants were observed, those concerned with the healthy development of children wanted to explain them. If it were possible to define which aspects of institutional group care were related to the babies' failure to thrive, future child care planning could avoid such practices.

Thus, it was suggested that maternal deprivation was the cause. Certainly, the institutional conditions did not provide the type of individual mothering that most babies cared for at home receive. This explanation has been widely accepted. It is interesting to find that it may have influenced the relationships of mothers at home with their children even more than it influenced the structuring of substitute child care programs. Unfortunately, these programs often are the victims of the lack of sufficient funding and educated staff.

Recently there have been attempts to define even more specifically the ingredients of a healthy psychological environment for infants. Along with an understanding and acceptance of the tremendous significance of the concept of maternal deprivation, there has also been a recognition of other influences on the developing infant as well.

The Concept of Sensory Deprivation

As the concept of maternal deprivation has been reexamined, other questions have been raised. One consideration is whether lack of stimulation from the physical environment along with the lack of stable caretakers may have played a role in the children's failure to develop. New research in the field of psychology was showing that without *stimulation* — the continued exposure of the senses to opportunities to see, hear, smell, touch, move — people lose contact with their surroundings and neither perceive nor act normally. This research thus suggested that *sensory deprivation* — the lack of ongoing, organized stimulation from the outside world — might also have contributed to the harmful quality of the institutional environment of the institutionalized infants.

Today, it is generally accepted that both close ties with a primary caretaker and interesting and stimulating physical surroundings are essential for the process of normal emotional, social, and cognitive development to take place. Caretakers, in particular, have a special role in helping the infant to process the stimulation from the outside world. They must make sure that he has neither too much nor too little stimulation. In other words, mothers help introduce their infants to outside stimulation as they are ready to handle it and use themselves to help organize it for them. For example, when there is too much noise around an infant, his mother may pick him up and, through bringing him close to her body, help "buffer" the distressing sounds for him. Or, if an infant seems restless, she may sooth him by singing softly, thus bringing sounds into his awareness.

The Concept of Maternal Overprotection

One force contributing towards the reexamination of the concept of maternal deprivation was the fact that it seemed to have been inappropriately applied to some situations. One of these in particular was that of most home-based mothers caring for their babies. Many such mothers, as a result of reading popular literature attempting to interpret the maternal deprivation studies, came to feel, along with many professionals, that the biological mother must be the only one involved in caring for her child. Mothers were also made to feel that they must have a "perfect" relationship with their babies. Mothers were told that otherwise the resultant deprivation to the child would result in devastating effects on his emotional development. For fear of somehow subjecting their children to the kinds of institutional conditions which had led to the formulation of the maternal deprivation concept, many mothers felt that they must carry on the same type of close, attentive relationship with their older children as they had appropriately done when the children were infants.

The results of these practices were described in research carried out by Dr. David Levy. He called this concept *maternal overprotection,* the maintaining of an overly intense, dependency-based relationship well past the time that it is developmentally appropriate for the child. Mothers who were overprotective out of guilt and self-consciousness about child rearing were reluctant to develop interests other than raising their children. Thus, they did not encourage them to gradually grow towards independence. These mothers did not require their children to do things on their own which were within their capabilities. The children were protected from having to take responsibility for their behavior. A teenager might still expect, for example, his mother to lay out his clothes for him or to cut his meat for him. Such children, who were "smothered" rather than mothered, did not develop the kinds of age appropriate skills necessary to get along in the world.

Maternal overprotection increases the probability that young preschool age children will not master the two next developmental tasks outlined by Erikson as part of the theory mentioned earlier. *The Eight Stages of Man* lists *autonomy,* a sense of self-determination, and initiative as necessary to the development of the young child.

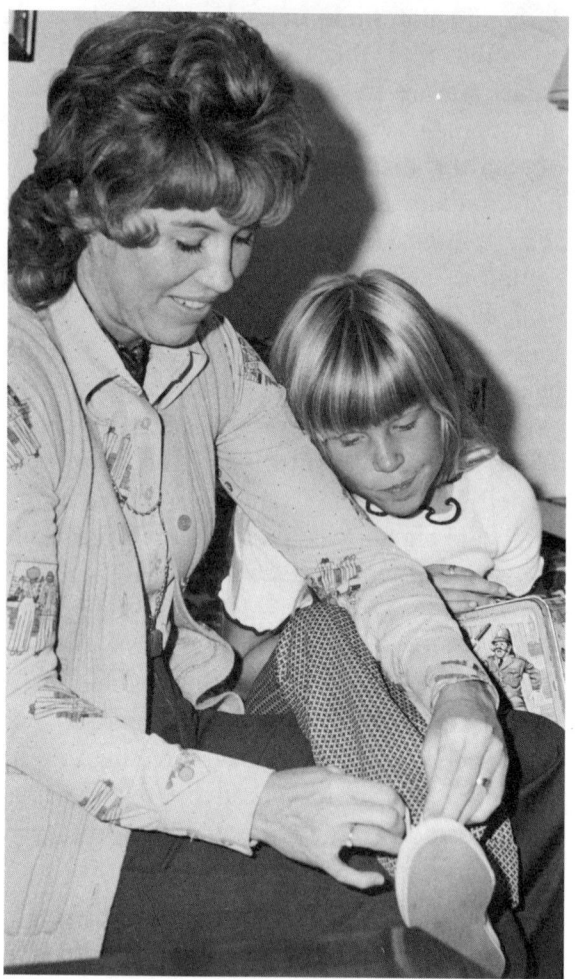

Neither extreme of the "mothering" dimension — maternal deprivation or maternal overprotection — is conducive to sound child development. Consideration of the factors of separation and timing contribute towards an understanding of the achievement of an appropriate balance between the two.

SEPARATION AND TIMING

The process of growth is a process of gradual separation. It has been shown that too early and too long separations from a mothering person during the earliest months and years of life are harmful. Failure to separate, in accordance with the rationale of maternal overprotection, is also detrimental to development. Recent researchers have

Unit 1 Factors Influencing Child Development

described the role of *detachment*. In this process, growing infants when they are physically ready gradually separate themselves from the object of their primary attachment. This puts them in touch with increased opportunity for learning and mastery as they are able to interact more with their physical environment. There is a developmental sequence to separation just as there is with attachment. At first, the exploring infant moves just a small distance away from his mother, keeping her in his sight and soon returning to her. Ainsworth has referred to this behavior appropriately as "exploration from mother as a secure base." In time, the child gradually moves further away from his mother and gradually permits himself to leave her out of sight.

The element of timing is important in considering the process of separation. The duration of separations is a factor that influences their effect on a child. If a child is separated from his primary caretaker for a long period of time, or experiences frequent separations, this naturally has a greater impact on him than brief or infrequent separations.

The age of an infant or small child is also crucial in considering the effect of separation. Greater effects are experienced by the younger child. Separation from the mother during the age range of three to twelve months is felt to be particularly unfavorable. This seems to be a critical period in the development of infants in terms of gaining a foundation for forming human relationships and for learning.

Older infants, around eight months old, show "separation anxiety" by crying when approached or handled by someone other than their mothers. This indicates that a strong bond of attachment has been formed. Children who have never developed such a bond do not react to separation from their caretakers. These are most likely to be those infants who show the severe apathy and developmental lags characteristic of human and environmental deprivation.

MULTIPLE MOTHERING

The significance of the close mother-child tie (uninterrupted by too early separations) has been discussed. It is important, however, to point out that this does not mean that others cannot be appropriately involved in caring for the infant. If a bond has been formed between the mother and infant, the help of others in caring for the child can be a positive experience for both mother and child.

Several people joining together to care for a child has been referred to as *multiple mothering*. The type of multiple mothering, however, in which there are several caretakers and the child does not have a special attachment to any one of them does not lead to positive development. There is some suggestion

7

that attachments are less strong when there are too many caretakers.

A series of interesting studies on monkey mothers was done by Kaufman. It indicates the positive benefit which can be experienced by mothers and infants with other adults present. Monkey mothers of one type cared for their infants in the company of many other female monkeys, who also interacted with them. When separated from their mother, these monkey infants not only did not become withdrawn, but also drew caring responses from the other female monkeys. In another type of monkey, however, the mothers isolated themselves from others with their infants. In these cases when separation took place, the infants became apathetic, and no other adult monkeys showed an inclination to take over their care.

THE ROLE OF THE FATHER

Traditionally, the father has not always played a major role in the direct care of small infants, but has served more as the family provider. Nonetheless, the role of the father in the life of the infant is a highly important one. This fact is increasingly recognized as the cultural definition of fatherhood is changed.

During the infant's early weeks, the father plays a special role. He provides support and shared strength to the mother as she adapts her activities to meeting the infant's many needs for round-the-clock care. The father may also take part in providing some direct care of the child. More and more fathers are finding joy in caring for their infants. Male involvement in the care of very young children is no longer felt to be unmasculine in the American culture.

Some fathers may feel awkward with a completely dependent, very tiny infant. These fathers begin to feel more comfortable when their children begin to crawl and toddle and, in general, show more strength and competence.

As the child begins to explore the world physically, he becomes more aware of his father's presence in his world and begins to develop a closer relationship with him. This helps the child begin to separate from his mother as he is ready. In the lives of most children raised in a family with both a mother and father present, the father becomes a most significant person in the child's life — second only to the mother.

When the father is present, the complementary roles and personalities of both mother and father are experienced. This happens at a time when the child is beginning to learn that there are different kinds of people in the world with whom he can have positive relationships. He may, for example, turn to his mother in times of special stress, but recognize the interest of his father at times when he is feeling active and playful. When the father takes part in the care of his young child from the start, the foundation is laid for the continuation of a highly significant relationship which will make many positive contributions to the child's overall development.

INDIVIDUALITY IN PSYCHOLOGICAL DEVELOPMENT

Each child meets general developmental tasks and responds to the environment provided by his caretakers, in his own individual way. Those who take care of children frequently hear such statements as, "All children are individuals." They also recognize from their own observations that different children may respond in varying ways to similar environmental experiences.

It is difficult, however, to respond in a constructive way to a vague concept of "individuality" without having an understanding of how it might specifically be related to children's behavior and development. Fortunately, recent research on *basic temperament* — a person's individual style of behavior or way of responding to the experience the world offers him — has provided a description of the role and nature of basic temperament, or individuality, in personality development.

As a result of a long term study, three researchers, Drs. Chess, Thomas, and Birch, isolated nine dimensions of basic temperament which seemed to be present from the time they were born in the children studied. These dimensions were (1) activity level, (2) biological regularity, (3) approach or withdrawal to a new situation, (4) adaptability to change in routine, (5) level of sensory threshold (sensitivity to change in sensory stimulation), (6) positive or negative mood, (7) intensity of response, (8) distractibility, and (9) attention span.

For example, from the day they were born, some babies were extremely active, moving around in their mothers' arms when picked up; others were quiet and placid. This indicated individual variations in the dimension of *activity level.* Some babies immediately got on a feeding schedule. Others wanted to be fed at one time during one day and at another time, the next day. These babies were showing differences in the dimension of *biological regularity.* On encountering a new food or a new face, some babies were interested and accepting; others, rejecting. Thus, these babies varied in the dimension of *approach-withdrawal to a new situation.*

All of these individual modes of response to the world reflected these children's basic temperament, or individuality. The research which described the various dimensions of individuality has several implications relevant to providing sound programming and care for young children.

First of all, it suggests that children are not only affected by the environment, but that through their individuality, they can shape the way others, such as parents or teachers, respond to them. For example, a caretaker will approach and handle a very active baby in a different way than she or he will a quiet, passive one. Without minimizing the role parents and prime caretakers play in enhancing their children's development, it can be seen that the quality of the relationship is not simply determined by these persons alone. It is the result of the child's characteristics in interaction with those of the adults who come in contact with him.

Then, results of the study indicate viewing and managing each individual child in a way that is related to his or her unique individuality, rather than by some preconception as to how he or she should behave. Sound child care practices build upon both the knowledge of what all children as a group require to have their needs met and upon what each child should have so that the environment responds to his unique individuality.

For the person working with young children, it is thus important to realize that the forces which shape the nature and destiny of each human individual are extremely complex. A healthy respect for this complexity is essential for the person whose goal is to promote positive development.

SUMMARY

This unit has described some basic processes in the relationship between infants, their individuality, their primary catetakers, and their physical environment. These must be recognized as fundamental to the design of substitute child care programs.

One way to describe the main developmental task of infancy is through the term *basic trust.* If the experience of the infant through the way in which he is cared for is positive, he emerges with a sense of the world as being a good place. The infant's development of a primary tie, or attachment, to a caretaking person is essential for achieving basic trust.

This attachment implies mutual interaction between the child and the caretaker, usually the mother. A contact initiated by one encourages a response from the other. The result is the continued development of a growth-producing relationship.

Studies of institutionalized infants who died or failed to thrive in infancy led to development of the concept of maternal deprivation. This describes a total lack of exposure to a person from whom an infant can receive individual care and attention. Maternal deprivation is more likely to take place when infants are given custodial care in groups, rather than when they are raised at home.

Sensory deprivation is now felt also to be accountable for the developmental problems observed in institutionalized infants. It is important also for infants to be exposed to interesting physical surroundings and to have the opportunity to explore them.

Separation as well as attachment is an important process in the development of the growing infant, when the separation is timed according to the infant's needs. Maternal overprotection describes a mode of care in which age-appropriate separation is not encouraged. This hinders the child in achieving the developmental tasks of initiative and autonomy. Involvement of others as participants in caring for an infant can be positive as long as the infant still develops a primary tie with one person. The father is more and more becoming an integral part of the life of his infant, both supporting the mother and participating in providing direct care to the child.

Dimensions of basic temperament describe the individual response patterns of children and need to be considered in order to provide individualized care for children.

SUGGESTED ACTIVITIES

- Visit a mother of an infant (aged four, six, or nine months old). Observe carefully the interaction between the mother and infant, noting how responses from each evoke responses from the other. Watch how she holds and speaks to the child, particularly when giving him basic care (feeding, changing, etc.). Consider your observations in relation to the concepts of basic trust and attachment and the age of the infant.

- Arrange to visit an institution or agency providing care for infants. Find out how many infants are cared for and what the staffing pattern is. How many staff are available to care for the children? How are they assigned to them? If you can, observe the physical surroundings of the setting. Where do the infants spend most of their time? What kinds of play materials and decorations are present? How do you feel the program meets the infants' needs for close attention and stimulation?

- Speak to the father of a newborn infant. Ask him how he feels about caring for his child and how he might expect his relationship with his child to continue to develop.

- Observe a small infant at home as he wakes up, is fed, and plays. Do you get a "feel" for his basic temperament? Is he characteristically active or passive? Does he follow a regular schedule? Does he seem highly sensitive or insensitive to changing levels of stimulation?

Compare your observations with those of his parents. Do they feel that he has responded consistently along these dimensions since birth? How do they feel his responses have affected the way they have cared for him?

REVIEW

A. Define each of the following.
   1. Basic trust
   2. Maternal deprivation
   3. Multiple mothering
   4. Attachment
   5. Sensory deprivation
   6. Basic temperament

B. Indicate the best choice to complete each of the following.
   1. Attachment
      a. Is a one way process.
      b. Continues in the same way throughout the child's life.
      c. Is a mutual process between parent and child.
      d. Is not important in the child's development.
   2. The concept of basic trust
      a. Specifies modes of child care which will help achieve it.
      b. Was described by Jean Piaget.
      c. Has the developmental outcome of the infant feeling positive about himself and the world.
      d. Is described as being unrelated to how the infant receives basic care.
   3. The results of Harlow's monkey studies suggest that the most important factor in promoting positive emotional development is
      a. Basic nourishment.
      b. Opportunity for intimate physical contact between infant and his caretaker.
      c. Opportunity for interaction with other youngsters.
      d. A large amount of sensory stimulation.
   4. All of the following are related to the concept of attachment except
      a. Attachment follows a developmental sequence.
      b. Basic temperament of both mother and child influences the quality of the attachment bond formed between them.
      c. During the attachment process, infants react in the same way to everyone.
      d. Continuity and consistency are important in developing attachment.

Section 1 Early Experience

5. Characteristics of babies raised in institutions were found to include all of the following except

   a. Rocking back and forth.
   b. Head banging.
   c. Repetitive behavior.
   d. Smiling.

6. A contemporary point of view is that lack of development observed in institutionalized infants was caused by

   a. Maternal overprotection and multiple mothering.
   b. Sensory deprivation and maternal deprivation.
   c. Sensory deprivation and maternal overprotection.
   d. Maternal deprivation and maternal overprotection.

7. The person who usually becomes most significant to a child as he begins to separate from his mother is the

   a. Closest brother or sister.
   b. Evening babysitter.
   c. Father.
   d. Grandmother.

8. It is felt that the separation of the child and primary caretaker is most likely to have an impact on the child if it takes place between the ages of

   a. One and four months.
   b. Nine and twelve months.
   c. Three and twelve months.
   d. Six and fifteen months.

9. A mother who is still tying the shoes of her ten-year-old daughter might be said to be demonstrating the concept of

   a. Maternal attachment.
   b. Multiple mothering.
   c. Early intervention.
   d. Maternal overprotection.

10. Johnny and Jimmy are brothers. When Johnny's mother used to pick him up to feed him, he would wiggle and wave his arms. When she picked Jimmy up, however, he would lie quietly in her arms. These boys were showing variations in the dimension of basic temperament called

    a. Attention span.
    b. Approach-withdrawal to new situation.
    c. Activity level.
    d. Level of sensory threshold.

unit 2 cultural influences on child rearing practices

OBJECTIVES

After studying this unit, the student should be able to

- Discuss the influence of cultural differences on the personality development of children.
- Describe the meaning of children to society and to parents in contemporary American culture.
- Describe the characteristics of both nuclear and extended family structures and their effects on child rearing practices.
- Describe the effect of mobility on families and children.
- Describe the differences in child rearing practices between the middle class and the working class.
- Discuss the characteristics of "inner city" culture and the strengths of the "inner city" child.

America is known as a *pluralistic* society. This means that its people share a variety of backgrounds and experiences. The various peoples who have settled America have each brought with them a common heritage, a common culture characteristic of the country or geographic area from which they came. For this reason, each cultural or "ethnic" group has its own particular way of viewing and dealing with life. This affects every aspect of daily living — where people live, what they eat, what they wear, what kind of work they choose to do, how they raise their children, and what they think is important in the world are all factors that influence their lives.

There can be great differences from group to group in these culturally determined "life styles" which affect the way children are viewed and raised. A family from one cultural background may feel, for example, that it is very important for everyone, including children, to be able to freely express their feelings. Another family, according to the practices of its culture, may feel that it is best for children to obey their parents without asking questions. A family from still another background may believe that it is best for children to work for the "extras" in their lives, while others may wish to give their children many of the material goods that they, themselves, did not have when they were children. In some cultures, children are expected to eat the foods served to them and to clean their plates. In others, children may be permitted to help themselves to food whenever they want it.

Cultural factors play an important part in shaping the ways in which people go about living and raising another generation. How any society or cultural group as a whole feels about children is extremely important in determining the kinds of child rearing practices which will be used both by parents and by child care programs. These practices, in turn, influence the kinds of adults the young grow up to be.

Section 1 Early Experience

Children in any group may come from diverse backgrounds, often different from that of the person caring for them. Thus, the teacher, the assistant, and others working with children must be able to understand and respond positively to the culturally-related behavior and attitudes of each child. How this is done affects how much benefit the child derives from the program and how he and his family feel about themselves as persons worthy of dignity and respect.

THE MEANING OF CHILDREN IN AMERICAN SOCIETY

In times past, childhood and adulthood were not considered to be separate stages of development. Children were regarded as physically smaller adults rather than as persons with particular needs and characteristics related to their age. Since the beginning of the twentieth century in America, however, childhood has been viewed as a developmental stage separate and different from adulthood.

In keeping with the recognition of the separateness of childhood, America has frequently been called a "child centered" society. The term suggests that a substantial amount of adult effort and resources are focused on providing a "good life" for young children. Unfortunately, statistics, as well as professional opinions, indicate that America does not really meet the diverse needs of its children.

Many children are being raised under circumstances destructive to positive development: poverty, lack of educational opportunity, inadequate physical care, and poor emotional climate. There are not enough child care programs available for the many children and their families who need them. Many of the child care programs are of poor quality, with a small trained staff and too little financial support.

The stress of various cultural groups in America on such values as having material

goods ("A TV in every window and a car in every garage"), on solving problems by force ("law and order"), on being able to get ahead ("by hard work"), and on being unable to cause the rich "establishment" to change, influence child care practices. Children receive messages from their parents and the others with whom they associate about which values and achievements in society are important.

A recent trend in American society which affects child rearing practices is that towards having smaller families. During pioneer days, large families were an economic necessity. Children were needed to help perform the work necessary for survival. In the years after World War II, with the return of soldiers to the work force, women again stayed home and concentrated on raising children. Large families were fashionable and considered a special means of female fulfillment. Today, as a result of the women's liberation movement, a concern with overpopulation, and other factors, many feel differently about family size. There is much less pressure on young couples to have large families, or, for that matter, to have any children at all.

THE MEANING OF CHILDREN TO FAMILIES

When a couple does have children, however, each child has a special meaning which helps shape the ways the child is reared. The meaning a child holds for his parents is further molded by the fact that becoming a parent in itself has a particular meaning in the life of the adult. Psychological growth and development of the human being does not end magically when the adolescent period (13-21) is past. Rather, the undertaking of parenthood is a developmental stage in itself. It requires an adjustment for adults not only of their lifestyle, or way of living, but also of their feelings about themselves and about children.

There are ways in which adults' relationships with their own parents influence the styles of care they adopt with their own children. They may not be especially aware of this, however. Becoming pregnant revives a future mother's feelings about her own mother. In turn, knowing he is to become a father revives a man's feelings about his own father. At the prospect of becoming parents, adults are stimulated to think back to their own childhoods. If they have happy memories, they may decide that they wish to raise their children the way they themselves were brought up. Parents' own recollections of childhood may be unpleasant. They may then deliberately plan to do things differently with their own children.

For those couples who actively are looking forward to having children, having a baby means that there will be a third person entering their lives. What was formerly a close union of just two people can no longer exist. *Ambivalent* (both positive and negative) feelings about becoming parents are normal. Society has created a myth that becoming parents of a new baby is sheer joy. It is now recognized and accepted that while prospective fathers and mothers have positive feelings of gladness and anticipation, they also have worries and concerns. A woman may wonder, for example, if she "will get her figure back," whether her husband's loving feelings for her will remain intact, and whether her child will be all right. An unmarried mother often has serious concerns about whether she should keep her child and how she will be able to support it. A father may wonder if he will be "tied down" too much, and whether his wife will still care as much about him with a new baby to tend.

There is a variety of specific meanings a child may have for its parents. To some mothers, a baby is the fulfillment of a childhood expectation and dream to someday be a mother. To others, a baby may represent an

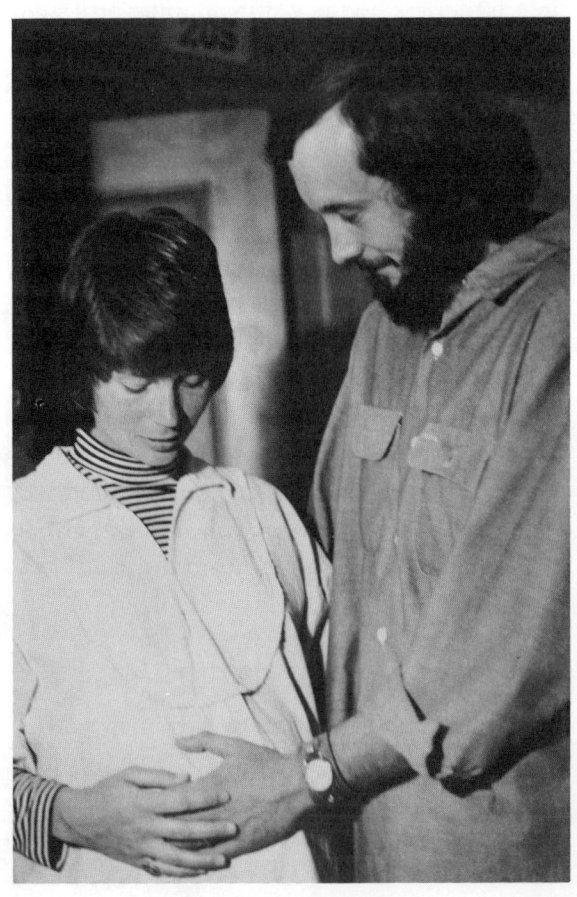

interruption in the opportunity to follow other interests. To one prospective father, a baby cements his feeling about himself as being a family man and provider. To another, it is a mouth to feed; to still another, the new baby will hopefully be a son — a longed for extension of himself.

To some families, the pregnancy occurs at the right time in their lives. Both parents may have completed their educations, advanced in their jobs, and acquired the finances they feel will be sufficient to support a larger family. Babies are born, also, to families having few resources. Perhaps the couple is young and married to get away from conflict within their own families. Neither may have the education to find a stable, adequately paying job.

It is one thing to be the firstborn baby of a couple living in a middle class neighborhood. It is quite another to be the sixth child in a fatherless household in an inner-city slum, to belong to a family living in a migrant worker camp, or to have a fourteen year-old school girl for a mother.

Sex and order in the family are two other factors influencing the way a family views and raises a particular child. Sometimes parents prefer one sex over the other. Whether a child is a firstborn or the last of six, (his "ordinal" position in the family) has an effect on his experiences within it.

Thus, the birth of a child is more than a physical event for a family. Becoming parents induces changes in both the outlook and way of living of the parents. This, in turn, affects the way in which they care for and raise the child.

AMERICAN FAMILY STRUCTURE

In a pluralistic society with many different subcultural groups, there are different ways of organizing and carrying out family life. Each of these family "contexts" has a different effect on the children living in them.

The two most predominant forms of family organization in America are identified by the terms *nuclear* and *extended.*

Many families, including most middle class (moderately well-off financially) families, are *nuclear*. This means that within one household there live only two generations: parents and children. *Extended* families, on the other hand, are those in which several generations may be represented under the same roof. Grandparents, cousins, aunts, and uncles, as well as last-generation parents and children, may live together. Nuclear families appeared following the Industrial Revolution. At that time, young people left their extended farm families to seek a living in cities and began their own separate families.

What are the effects of nuclear family living? First of all, it can create a sense of isolation. This is often true of young mothers who are left alone in the house when their husbands go to work. Regardless of how much they love their families and children, they are apt to feel lonely. It is not really a "normal" situation for one mother and one child to be alone together in a house for a full day. It is better for the mother's mental health, as well as for her ability to foster that of her child, to somehow have contacts and links with the outer world.

Emotions in the nuclear family may be more intense than those in an extended family. When a mother and child have contact with few other people within the household during the course of a day, all the interaction which takes place is naturally between the mother and child. It is seldom tempered by the input from others. There is a need for "buffering" feelings to prevent them from growing overly intense. For example, a mother may be having "a bad day" and may be gloomy and irritable. These feelings are much more likely to be expressed in the way she cares for her child if she is alone than they would be if there were an aunt, cousin, or other adult who could talk to the mother and help care for the child during this time.

During infancy, it is necessary for a strong bond to be established between the child and a mother person, as was mentioned in the preceding unit. This does not mean that others cannot participate in the ongoing life of the mother and child, however.

In contemporary America, most middle class and upper class (high income) families are nuclear in structure. Exceptions include single parent families, families in which there is a live-in substitute caretaker, and families which live in groups or communes. Many nuclear families include first generation college graduates who have left home to establish careers in the cities or growing suburbs. Inner city families may be either nuclear or extended. Extended families are still found among particular *ethnic* (representative of a particular country or culture) groups and among recent immigrant families. In these cases, the young generation joins older relatives who have already established themselves.

MOBILITY AS A CULTURAL FACTOR IN FAMILY LIFE

Mobility, or frequent moving, is an important characteristic of American society today and exerts a significant influence on family living styles and the ways children are brought up. "Mommy, what's a home town?" is a question that was asked by a child who is the product of a family which has moved frequently as a result of the father's job transfers.

The disruptive effects of frequent moving on children and their families are felt in the loss of a sense of continuity and of security. Mobile families may never get to know their neighbors well enough to share different aspects of each others' lives. The old fashioned guidance, support, and friendship that adult neighbors could offer children in "the olden days" as part of a shared adult responsibility for raising society's young, seldom any longer take place. No sooner do the children make friends and become used to a new school, than they must move and begin the same process all over again.

Some children and families adapt to mobility more readily than others. Certain individuals may thrive on frequent moves. They enjoy meeting new people and tackling different situations. They may develop a useful flexibility from mastering these challenges. For many, however, there are some general types of problems which emerge as a result of frequent moves. First of all, the mother may experience a strong sense of isolation. She must — if not employed — deal with strange people and surroundings. At the same time, the father makes new friends on the job with others who share his interests. A mother who is herself lonely may have trouble in helping her children become "established" in a new place. She often finds herself responsible for making most of the decisions about the children. She is also the one who "disciplines" them if the father's job requires long hours or frequent absences. Sometimes this situation creates difficulty in parent-child relations. The children may come to see the mother as the "bad" person. The father, unentangled in the difficulties of their everyday lives, may be seen as the "good" one.

To help counteract some of the negative effects on family life of "corporate" mobility, many large corporations are now taking steps to reduce the number of times they ask an executive to move. It seems, however, that mobility, "corporate" or not, will be a way of life for many families. The persons who work with children need to recognize the by-products of the feelings of uprootedness and lack of continuity it causes.

Section 1 Early Experience

 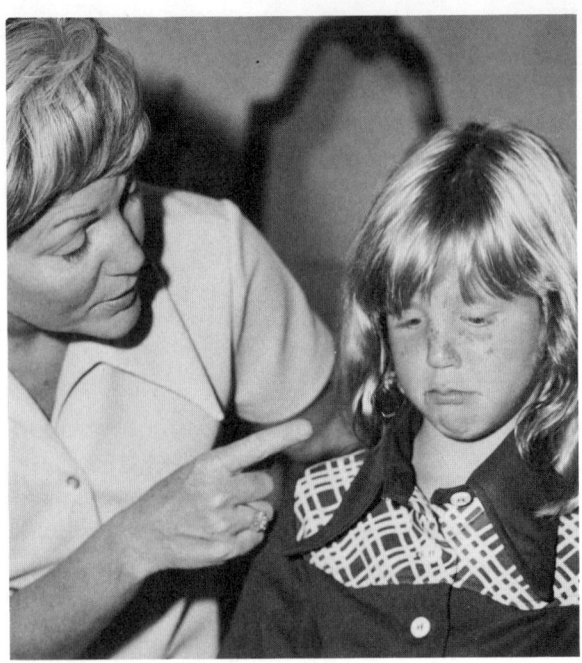

THE EFFECT OF ECONOMIC CLASS ON CHILD REARING PRACTICES

Studies show that the general income level at which a family lives is related to its overall "life-style." Consequently, the attitudes of the family towards ways of raising children are also affected.

"Middle" class parents — persons with a comfortable income, a high level of education, and frequently professionals — often employ what some term "liberal" child rearing practices. As a group, they may be less strict and rigid than those in a lower income, working class situation. In fact, the area of discipline is probably the greatest area of differences between the two groups. Middle class parents are more likely to feed their infants on "demand" schedules, to be casual about toilet training, and to be self-conscious about the way they are doing things.

Lower class parents, on the other hand, live with the difficulties of limited income, lack of other supports, and even limited space. As a result, they may want to urge their children more quickly along towards independence. Thus, they may wean their children earlier; they may begin toilet training early. They are less likely to read the many manuals on child rearing which are available and to take time to reflect on the way they are doing things.

Middle class parents generally permit more expression of feelings, even negative ones such as anger, on the part of their children. They are apt to be more tolerant of disobedience. Lower class parents, on the other hand, may expect their children to comply readily to adult authority, without question and without explanation. They may also have more difficulty accepting a child's impulses or *regressive behavior* (behavior characteristic of children at earlier stages of development). When a child does misbehave, lower class parents are more likely to use physical punishment than reasoning or redirection of behavior to guide him. Middle class parents, according to some studies, have been found to speak to their children and to praise their efforts more than do lower class parents.

It should be pointed out that not all middle class parents are "permissive" and that not all lower class ones are rigid in their child rearing practices. Some characteristics related to one group may be present in some individuals in the other group.

It should be recognized also that lower class parents, particularly those in the lowest income brackets, must raise their children under very difficult circumstances related to their lack of income. This imposes stresses which naturally make it more difficult for them to take time to explain things to their children or to accept behavior which is trying. Middle class parents often have more space and storage areas in their homes. Here, children can roam about more, but are less likely to break something. Mothers in favorable income circumstances may have help in keeping things clean and space to allot to children's activity. For these reasons, they can accept messy activities more readily. If something is destroyed in a low income household, there may be no money to replace it. Middle class parents may simply be able to buy an item to replace the one that was destroyed.

INNER CITY CULTURE

Children of poverty-level families living in slum areas of cities are sometimes referred to as "inner city" children. Such children have also been described as "culturally deprived" or "disadvantaged." Many people have disagreed with the accuracy of these terms, which seem to denote an inferiority that does not actually exist in the children. As a result of their particular life experiences, these children may be different. They are not necessarily inadequate in comparison to children living in other areas in families of larger income.

These children began to receive attention when it became recognized that many slum-raised children, upon reaching school age, had difficulty in achieving in traditional school subjects. It was felt that this was due to the fact that their poverty-level living conditions prevented them from having enriched early experiences. Such experiences supposedly are provided by middle class families for their children and seem to be the necessary foundation for later success in school learning.

Inner city life can indeed be grim and difficult. More and more middle class families become discouraged with life there and move to the suburbs where there is more space, new housing, and "better schools." The low income families are still left in the inner city. Others also migrate there from other areas, such as the South or the West Indies, and occupy decaying housing left by others. This, naturally, does not contribute to the "good life", nor does it make family life and child rearing pleasant and easy. Even where *urban renewal* — the tearing down of large segments of old housing and putting up large new apartment buildings — has taken place, it has not always improved the comfort and functioning of those who live there. Inner city housing, whether it is old or new, is often flimsy, cramped, and poorly laid out.

One difficulty of the newer housing projects has been in providing play space for children. It is difficult, for example, for children to have active, outdoor play when they live on the twelfth floor of a housing project. Such housing, when it is poorly planned and designed, also contributes to the break up of subcultural and neighborhood groups. Even if they lived in shabby quarters, these people formerly were able to have close "neighborly" contact with each other. The physical structure of the newer housing contributes towards isolation of families from one another.

The inner city, poverty-level family follows a life-style geared towards sheer survival. Continual effort must be expended to get enough food to live on, particularly if it is overpriced by exploitative market owners and lacks nourishment value, or to get enough warm clothes for the children to wear so they can attend school. Health services are difficult to obtain. There are long waiting lines in clinics. Appointment times are not kept. Sometimes the attitudes of the staff rob the patients of their dignity and self-respect. Home maintenance is difficult. Landlords may complain that tenants do not take care of property. However, shabby, overpriced housing does not encourage its occupants to feel like caring for it.

Time for the inner city families who are on public assistance is often punctuated by the arrival of the welfare check. Welfare benefits are helpful to the families that receive them. However, there is often much "red tape" associated with receiving the benefits. It may be easier, for example, for a middle class person to buy new glasses than it is for a person on welfare to get them — even though public assistance pays for them.

All of these difficulties in daily survival contribute towards a climate in which there is depression and little hope. The pleasures of life which others take for granted are not experienced by inner city families. It follows that there will be a greater amount of violence and more domestic problems. Children may witness angry fights, alcoholism, drug abuse, and even killings.

Some researchers have characterized the predominant inner city culture as being *matriarchal*. Families are headed by the mother rather than the traditional father. Although others do not agree with this, it does seem as if the effects of such life circumstances — the cycle of poor education, poor employment or lack of employment — have contributed to the instability of the nuclear family in the inner city. Sometimes welfare rules seem to contribute. A man earning less than his family would gain in welfare payments may deliberately leave so that his family can have the increased financial aid available if there is no male head of the house.

Child care for mothers who are the sole parent is difficult. While there has been progress made in establishing child care centers for poverty level families, there still are not enough. Often such parents have the additional burden of making "makeshift" arrangements. These may range all the way from leaving a child with a neighbor or grandparent to leaving him alone or with brothers and sisters barely older than he is.

Black people living in the inner city have experienced particular hardship. Members of other immigrant groups at least have not suffered severe economic, employment, and social discrimination. The racism which blacks have experienced has served not only to lock many into a poverty cycle, but also to show lack of recognition for their particular culture and style of living. Cultural differences between black children and the middle class staff members of inner city schools have detracted from the educational force of the school. They have also made it more difficult for such children to develop skills and interests which would increase their job and educational opportunities. Even with skills and with the advances in racial equality achieved in the sixties, blacks find barriers to following the inner-city suburban movement pattern of whites of varying ethnic backgrounds. This in turn perpetuates a vicious cycle of poverty and despair.

Some adults who work with young children may never have experienced poverty or

slum life or worked with inner city children and families. They should attempt to bear in mind the relationship that exists between the hardships of such a life and the ways children from these backgrounds are being raised. If a teacher is to be successful in working with young children and their families, she must understand and relate to them in terms of their environment and experiences, not her own. For example, their language style and usage may be different than that of the teacher or the assistant and of the middle class children. The fact that some inner city children may not use what is called "standard English" may cause communication problems. This does not mean that their language is less adequate than that of their middle-class counterparts.

The strengths of such children and families must be recognized. Inner city children have resources that many middle class children do not have a chance to develop. By necessity, they may be more independent. They can take care of themselves and even perform household tasks and other activities necessary to keep a family going. They may be much more resourceful in a crisis situation, knowing how to get themselves "out of a spot." Eisenberg is a scholar who has studied and described the strengths of inner city children. He feels they may be more concerned with helping each other than with competition, which is often a destructive preoccupation of the middle class child. The doing style which these children need in order to survive is shown by their physical skills and response to action oriented learning situations and tasks. The person working with inner city children should be able to recognize these strengths and help each child build upon them.

CULTURE AND INDIVIDUALITY

Cultural factors, as they affect the nature of child rearing practices, are related to the ways children develop. It is important to bear in mind, however, that every child has an individual, unique personality. Within any culturally determined subgroup, each person has his own personal style and way of viewing and dealing with the world.

SUMMARY

Child rearing practices and, therefore, the way children develop into adults are strongly influenced by cultural characteristics. There are many culturally based differences in the way American children are raised. It is important that those helping with the care of young children recognize this in order to most effectively understand and work with the diverse children they may encounter. At the same time, they must recognize that individual personalities vary greatly in any culturally determined subgroup.

Although American society claims to place a high value on children, there are many children being brought up today whose needs are not being met. Societal trends such as those toward having small families and many material goods influence the "message" American families give their children.

Children mean different things to individual families. Having a baby often causes new parents to think back to the way they were cared for as children and marks their entrance into a new developmental stage. It is recognized that negative feelings are normal in prospective parents.

One way of characterizing American family structure is through the terms *nuclear family* and *extended family*. There are advantages and disadvantages to each of these family patterns in terms of child raising.

A particular feature of American family life is frequent mobility (moving). This makes it difficult for people to feel they have "roots." This can cause psychological hardship to families.

Section 1 Early Experience

Families with adequate incomes — middle class families — are able as a group, to be more flexible in their child rearing practices than are poor lower class families. Inner city children live in slums and in families shut off from economic, educational, and social opportunity. The pattern of their housing contributes towards making their life difficult. Minority families in the inner city suffer the additional handicap of prejudice and discrimination. Inner city children have many strengths — resourcefulness, independence, and physical skills — which are more advanced than those of middle class children.

SUGGESTED ACTIVITIES

- Watch a morning of children's T.V. programs — the Saturday cartoons. What do these programs and the commericals which are also shown tell you about American culture? How do you think these programs, as a cultural characteristic, affect children?

- Talk to the parents of a firstborn new baby. Ask them how they felt when they knew they were going to have a child. Ask them by what values they plan to raise their children.

- Locate a nuclear and an extended family, and see if you can arrange to spend the better part of a day with each one. Observe who takes care of the small children in each family. Ask the mother in the extended family what it means to her in terms of caring for the children to have family relatives living with her.

- Many cities have an organization called "Welcome Wagon" to help new families learn about the resources of the city. If there is one near you, contact it. Ask if you can find out more about its activities and the reasons for them. How can such an organization help the "mobile" family?

- Go to any area where family and children's activities are held — beach, zoo, park. Tactfully observe families in their activities. See if you can identify "class-related" child rearing practices among those you watch. Compare the way different families handle the same situation.

- Go to a park or play area near an "inner city" neighborhood. Watch groups of children at play. Describe their play in terms of what it shows about the strengths of such children.

REVIEW

A. Define each of the following.

1. Ethnic
2. Culture
3. Subculture
4. Life-style
5. Pluralistic
6. Ambivalence
7. Nuclear family
8. Extended family
9. Mobility

B. Indicate the best choice for each of the following.

1. In America
   a. There is only one culture and way of raising children.
   b. There are two basic cultures.
   c. There are many different subcultures and ways families view children.
   d. Cultural factors have no influence on child rearing practices.

2. All of the following statements about childhood and adulthood today are considered to be true except
   a. They are separate stages of development.
   b. They are related to each other in that child rearing practices affect adult personality.
   c. They have the same developmental characteristics.
   d. How they were cared for during childhood influences prospective parents' feelings about having and raising children.

3. Prospective parents are most likely to feel all of the following except
   a. Complete, sheer joy at the prospect of having a baby.
   b. Fears that their "life-style" will become more restricted.
   c. Worries that their spouses' attitudes toward them may change.
   d. Both happiness and concern.

4. All of the following are characteristic of the nuclear family except
   a. Mothers may feel isolated.
   b. Feelings between mother and child may be intense.
   c. Relatives are readily available to give advice and support.
   d. Fathers usually work away from the home.

5. Mobile families
   a. Experience a sense of continuity.
   b. Sometimes have discipline problems with their children.
   c. Develop close supportive ties with their neighbors.
   d. Have no problems related to frequent moving.

6. Mrs. Jones and Mrs. Smith both have eighteen-month-old children. Mrs. Jones does not get upset when Jimmy has a toilet accident. She simply changes his clothes. She talks to him frequently even though he does not always appear to respond. When she is puzzled about him, she reads a child rearing book. Mrs. Smith becomes concerned when Johnny has an accident, speaks to him in brief phrases, and does not own a book on child rearing.
   a. Both are most likely "upper class" parents.
   b. Both are most likely "lower class" parents.
   c. Mrs. Jones is "middle class" and Mrs. Smith is "lower class."
   d. Mrs. Jones is "lower class" and Mrs. Smith is "upper class."

7. Some housing projects have caused difficulty for inner city families for all of the following reasons except
   a. It is difficult to take children downstairs to play from a top floor apartment.
   b. New housing broke up old neighborhood groups.
   c. Construction has sometimes been shoddy and flimsy.
   d. The external appearance of the units is unpleasant.

8. Compared to suburban or middle class children, inner city children
   a. Are less likely to view violence and domestic problems.
   b. Are less independent and resourceful.
   c. Lack physical skills.
   d. Are less competitive.

9. Johnny refuses a dish of beets served for lunch at nursery school. A reason which should be particularly considered for his doing this is
   a. He may not have been exposed to beets previously in his family.
   b. He is being stubborn and resisting his teacher.
   c. He is not very hungry.
   d. He wants dessert.

Section 2 Early Intervention

unit 3 the concept of early intervention

OBJECTIVES

After studying this unit, the student should be able to

- Describe the evolution of the concept of early intervention.
- Define the terms *culturally deprived* and *disadvantaged*.
- Define and describe the concept of early intervention.
- Define the concepts of prevention, compensation, enrichment, and custodial care.
- Describe the significance of nutrition in child development.
- Discuss the developmental rationale underlying early intervention programs.
- Describe the common factors that exist among early intervention, stimulation, and interpersonal relationships.

Programs and services for young children have existed for years. One major purpose has been to provide children with essential care which for some reason their parents cannot. Another has been to give them additional exposure to the kinds of experiences their parents want for them.

Only since the 1960s, has a strong movement been under way to examine the ability of programs to promote the optimal development of essentially normal children. No longer are services for children viewed either as ways to simply "take care" of them while their parents are absent, or to provide "extras" for children who already are receiving many of the experiences contributing to healthy growth. Today, children's programs and services are being carried out on the basis of their ability to intervene in a positive way — to affect the course of children's overall development.

25

Section 2 Early Intervention

EVOLUTION OF THE CONCEPT OF EARLY INTERVENTION

With the recognition more than a decade ago that many of the nation's children were lagging behind in overall development and basic educational skills at the time they started elementary school, a new emphasis was placed on the significance of early experience in child development. It was felt that many children who were not succeeding in school might be helped to better achievement if efforts to stimulate their acquisition of necessary learning skills were made prior to the time for them to begin school.

The children who were the main targets of this concern were primarily from poverty and inner city backgrounds. It was suggested that the life experiences and general environments of such children lacked the ingredients which usually contribute to the development of *cognitive* (intellectual) skills and the ability to master reading and other academic activities. These children were initially designated as *culturally deprived*. This term meant that their daily lives, or the culture in which they were raised, somehow lacked emphasis on the experiences which provide a background for school learning skills.

The experiences these children lacked might, for example, include exposure to creative media and play materials (such as blocks, paints, manipulative toys), to music, and to a wide variety of people and activities in the community. They might also involve close attention from adults involving encouragement to play and verbal interaction about all of the children's activities. Such activities are considered to be the kinds of learning experiences for young children which provide the foundation of general knowledge and language skills.

Criticism was leveled against the use of the term "culturally deprived." Some felt it implied that these poverty and inner city children "were missing something" — that they were deficient in comparison to middle class children. The suggestion was made that perhaps these children should be viewed as merely different — with different backgrounds and educational needs. Therefore, more recently, the term *disadvantaged* has been used to refer to children living in poverty and slum areas. This term more accurately relates lack of opportunity to economic rather than cultural factors. Critics of the term "culturally deprived" point out that these children do have a culture — one closely associated with the conditions imposed on their families as they try to survive under conditions of great hardship. Such a culture is also seen as contributing

26

many strengths to the children raised in it, as was pointed out.

Recognition of cultural differences did not, in the eyes of many, change the fact that the children who are labeled disadvantaged do seem to lack the particular skills in language and abstraction necessary for achievement in the school system. Therefore, a nationwide effort was mounted. It had two major purposes. The first was to define specifically the kinds of early experiences which are necessary to facilitate children's later educational achievement. The next was to design and carry out the kinds of programs which provide these experiences to the children who need them.

Tremendous financial backing for this effort was provided by the federal government. The Economic Opportunity Act of 1964 provided for the creation of Project Head Start, designed to provide disadvantaged children with a "head start" for beginning school, through a program of socializing and stimulating experiences. Later, in 1967, Title IV-A and IV-B of the Social Security Act were appended to support the provisions of day care (all-day child care programs). The main function of day care was to offer needed safe group care for children of working parents. However, strong interest emerged in also having the curriculum of these programs as helpful as possible in the total development of the children being cared for.

The programs mentioned above and many other program models which have been subsequently developed in the recognition of new and emerging needs are referred to as *early intervention*. The following section defines and describes this and related concepts. They all outline the thinking behind many contemporary early childhood programs.

EARLY INTERVENTION AND RELATED CONCEPTS

Intervention is, according to a definition proposed by Siegel, Secrist, and Forman[1], "a conscious and purposeful set of actions intended to change or influence the anticipated course of development." In this sense, a variety of contemporary educational and health oriented activities can be considered to be interventive. Thus, an "intervention" might be an educational program, planned medical care, special supports offered to parents, or many other similar activities intended to alter an established course of development so that it may proceed along a more positive track. To many in the field of early childhood education today, however, the term intervention refers primarily to the large number of programs which have been implemented in recent years to serve disadvantaged children and their families. Many interventive programs, which are described in detail in the next unit, include the provision of health care and assistance for parents, as well as educationally oriented activities for children.

To most effectively express the meaning of intervention, it is necessary to examine several related concepts. One of the most important of these is *prevention*. Prevention is, pehaps, the ultimate goal of intervention. In the field of human services, three forms of prevention are recognized.[2] *Primary prevention* is designed to prevent a disorder from developing at all. *Secondary prevention* is geared towards reducing the "duration and prevalence (i.e., the total number of cases) of those disorders which do occur." In other words, secondary prevention means modifying

---

[1] I. Siegel, A. Secrist and G. Forman, "Psycho-educational Intervention Beginning at Age Two: Reflections and Outcomes," In J. Stanley, ed. *Compensatory Education for Children Ages 2-8*, Baltimore: The Johns Hopkins University Press, 1973.

[2] J.W. Kessler, *Psychopathology of Childhood*, Englewood, N.J.: Prentice-Hall, 1966, p. 487.

a deviation or problem at a very early stage in its formation. *Tertiary prevention* is the specific treatment of an obvious handicap or disorder. Tertiary prevention, Kessler points out, is similar to rehabilitation. It provides assistance to a disabled person in order that he can develop to his fullest and live the most normal life possible. All types of prevention are served by interventive programs.

A major reason for lowering the age at which children are served by interventive programs is to reach them at an age when primary prevention is possible. This is undoubtedly the most effective intervention — more effective than waiting until children are older. At that time there would be a greater likelihood of impairment necessitating intervention as tertiary prevention only.

Intervention in early childhood is usually initiated through an effort to structure specific types of programs and expose children to them. Examination of several concepts developed to describe such programs extends the understanding of the meaning of intervention.

A *custodial program* for children is one which simply provides physical care for children when their parents are not available. It is sometimes acknowledged as being similar to baby sitting. The children must be kept safe and their basic physical needs met. A *remedial program* is one which is designed to correct specific problems or deviations which are established and obvious such as physical handicaps, speech problems, reading inadequacies, and others. Most interventive early childhood programs are primarily neither of these. Rather, they are *compensatory* which means they are intended to make up for, or *compensate* for, present lacks in children's functioning. They do this by offering relevant activities and experiences which the children have missed earlier.

In general, compensatory programs are considered to be large scale attempts to influence the development of disadvantaged children rather than a means of remediation for a specific handicap. The Head Start program is frequently described as compensatory. The specific curricula of compensatory programs are varied. Some may utilize *enrichment* — the provision of activities designed to be more encompassing, more intensive, and more extensive, than those the children customarily experience; others are more directly educational, attempting to directly teach academic skills.

DEVELOPMENTAL RATIONALE OF EARLY INTERVENTION PROGRAMS

A well designed program for children always has a *rationale* — reasons for being and for being a particular way. The reasons which comprise the rationale for an early intervention program derive from its basic goal — to provide experiences that make up for previous deficits in the children's lives. In this way, it is hoped that the children may be more likely to achieve their full potential.

The following basic premises of development are related to the rationale of early intervention.

- **Early experience is highly important.** One of the major premises underlying interventive preschool programming is that the quality of children's early experience is crucial in terms of determining the course of later development. Thus, improving the quality of that experience can be beneficial. If early experience were not important, there would be no reason for trying to alter its characteristics. There is debate concerning which aspects of early experience are the most crucial and the permanence and nature of their effect. Almost all who study human development agree, however, that the first years of life hold tremendous significance in determining the course and nature of future development.

- **The quality of the environment plays a role in determining cognitive ability.** Few people now hold to the age-old belief that intelligence is completely inherited — that it is determined genetically and set unchangeably at birth. If this old belief were so, it would mean that experiences provided by their environment would be of little importance in determining the level of children's intellectual functioning. On the other hand, it has been found that the quality of early relationships and stimulation as provided environmentally bears a strong relationship to children's development of cognitive skills.

- **Nutrition is an important factor related to environmental influences on development.** It is increasingly recognized that there is a strong relationship between nutrition and mental ability. There is evidence that chronic poor nutrition, a frequent accompaniment of poverty status, negatively influences the development of the brain and central nervous system. This, in turn, may be reflected in decreased intellectual ability.

  The poorly nourished child may be apathetic (withdrawn) at a time when an adequate activity level is essential for development to proceed normally. The active, alert child is able to interact with his environment and receive feedback from it which continues to stimulate him and furthers his learning. The child who is listless as the result of poor health or nutrition just does not have the energy to interact in a positive way with his environment.

  The significance of nutrition in relationship to psychological as well as physical development provides new insight into the issue of the role of the environment in child development. If nutrition, including the nutritional status of a mother-to-be and the quality of nutrients she is thus able to provide the fetus, influences the potential for intellectual growth of an infant, then nutrition, rather than genetic (inherited) factors, may be related to level of intellectual ability. For populations which have lived in poverty with its resultant malnourishment over generations, this is particularly applicable. Thus, major interventive and preventive programs which promote positive development of young children must assure adequate nutrition for both mothers and children.

- **There are critical periods for learning.** Closely related to the significance of the environment for cognitive development is that of the *critical period*. This means that there are crucial times or points in the growth of human beings at which they are particularly open to learning certain skills or concepts and to profiting from relevant experiences which might encourage this particular learning. Benjamin Bloom has been widely quoted for his work suggesting that by the age of four, children have developed approximately one-half of their intelligence, and by the age of six, nearly two-thirds.[3] If this is indeed so, it provides a strong rationale for the establishment of interventive programs. These would offer experiences oriented towards encouraging intellectual development at the crucial times at which children's minds are developing the most rapidly and are the most open to influence.

- **Children have a strong motivation for mastery.** Results of studies of human

[3] M. Pines, *Revolution in Learning,* New York: Harper & Row, 1966.

behavior seem to indicate that people, children included, have an inner drive to learn and to master their environment. They are motivated to develop competence in new activities and skills through practice and exposure to new experiences. Terms which have been applied to these or similar processes include Robert White's *competence motivation* and J. McV. Hunt's *intrinsic motivation.* Hunt, in addition, has demonstrated a strong commitment to the value of interventive preschool programming.[4] The urge to master the environment bears an important relationship to learning and, therefore, to early intervention. It is a circular process. The more a child is exposed to opportunities for mastery, the more he learns. The more he learns, the more he continues to strive for mastery and further learning. When the environment does not provide stimulation and the opportunity to encourage the practice of new skills, children's motivation and resultant learning are diminished. Early intervention programs are believed to provide the kinds of stimulation and encouragement children need in order to sustain the motivation for mastery which is so crucial to their continued development of learning skills.

RELATIONSHIPS AND STIMULATION IN EARLY INTERVENTION

Specific models of early intervention programs offer a large range of activities and experiences. There are, however, several essentials in almost any interventive program. These include adequate nutrition and health care as well as organized stimulation in an interpersonal context. Before the wave of concern over cognitive development was generated in the 1960s, it was felt that the greatest benefit to young children of close and nurturing relationships with parent and other significant figures was primarily in emotional and social development. More recent research indicates that the quality of interpersonal relationships has a definite effect on intellectual development, particularly in the area of language skills. This research (such as Hess and Shipman's well known work on maternal teaching styles) indicates that parents actually are teachers as well as socializers and that their approach to their children bears a relationship to how well the children learn. Several kinds of parental behavior have been found to be related to early cognitive development. These include overall attentiveness to children, speaking to them, and responding to their attempts to speak back. Also, it is helpful for parents to give of themselves, reacting to children's activities with praise and encouragement.

As prime caretakers, parents provide stimulation to their children. They also play another important role with reference to stimulation; they are the "modifiers" of that stimulation. Lack of stimulation, in and of

---

[4] J. McV. Hunt, "The Psychological Basis for Using Preschool Enrichment as An Antidote for Cultural Deprivation," Passow, et. al., eds. *Education of the Disadvantaged: A Book of Readings,* New York: Holt, Rinehart and Winston, 1967.

itself, was pinpointed earlier as the "deficiency" in homes of children showing indications of deprivation. More recent scrutiny has altered this premise. It is now felt that rather than simply lacking stimulation, the problem may be that some children are exposed to unorganized stimulation. Examples of this may be a constant barrage of noise, such as a television set blaring hour after hour; a crib literally filled with stuffed animals; a noisy and flashy mobile always over the crib; and a noisy gathering of adults. This kind of thing overwhelms children's poorly developed sensory apparatus so that they develop "defenses" against the onslaught of distressing input which they are not capable of processing. As a result, they may become withdrawn and avoid people. They sometimes become overactive and have difficulty concentrating on only one thing. They may actually close themselves off from further constructive experiences because they find them too painful.

The encouragement of cognitive development, as well as social development, does not mean the unmodified provision of stimulation. Instead, stimulation should be provided and "monitored" by a person who has a close relationship with the child and who knows his sensitivities. Stimulation which would be too upsetting can be screened out, and only that which the child is developmentally ready to accept can be allowed in. For example, the person caring for the baby could hold him close when they had to be in a noisy group, and the television set could be turned off if the baby's crib could not be moved away from it.

Those who implement early intervention programs assume that stimulation is essential for promoting development. Those who work with well designed programs proceed on the premise that stimulation must be provided within the context of meaningful interpersonal relationships, adequate physical health, and the children's individual needs.

SUMMARY

Early intervention has grown out of the activities of the 1960s which indicated that many children were entering school without the background of knowledge and skills necessary for successful achievement. Programs of intervention, designed to provide during the preschool years the kinds of experiences which would better prepare children for later schooling, were mounted on a nationwide basis. Intervention, as an attempt to encourage positive development, is different from its related concepts of prevention and remediation. Programs designed to serve an interventive function have often been termed compensatory to "make up" for previous deficiencies in children's experience. There are a number of developmental principles which provide a rationale for intervention programs and influence their design. These include the significance of early experience, the quality of the environment (including nutrition) in determining level of intellectual development, the concept of "critical periods," and motivation for mastery. Organized stimulation in an interpersonal context is an essential provision of interventive programming.

SUGGESTED ACTIVITIES

- Arrange to visit two different types of preschool programs: a Head Start program and a "therapeutic" preschool for emotionally disturbed youngsters or a preschool for handicapped or retarded children. Compare the programs in the two settings. Try to identify those aspects of each which speak to the activities of intervention, prevention,

Section 2 Early Intervention

remediation, and compensation. Which program seems to fit most closely the definition of intervention?

- Observe unobtrusively mothers of infants, toddlers, and preschoolers in settings such as the park or supermarket. Focus on the way they speak to their children and respond to their children's attempts to communicate to them. Which mother's behavior observed do you feel will make the greatest contribution to the cognitive development of her child?

- Visit a toy store and ask to see the playthings for infants. Which do you think would be truly helpful to infants in learning to master the environment? Which do you think might simply intrude on the child with stimulus properties which he may not have the sensory development to handle?

- Observe some economically disadvantaged children at play. Do you feel that their play represents lack of experience or experience which is merely different from that of "middle class" children?

- Observe a toddler as he explores his environment. What do you think he is learning? How does his behavior relate to the concept of "motivation for mastery?"

- Plan to meet with a nutritionist who works with children's programs. What does this person feel the relationship is between the nutritional status of children and their learning ability? What services are provided to meet the nutritional needs of the children and their families?

REVIEW

A. Define each of the following.
 1. Intervention
 2. Primary, secondary, and tertiary prevention
 3. Enrichment
 4. Remediation
 5. Compensatory
 6. Culturally deprived
 7. Disadvantaged
 8. Critical period
 9. Motivation for mastery

B. Indicate the best choice for each of the following.
 1. The Head Start program was originally legislated into being and funded by
    a. Title IV A of the Social Security Act.
    b. The Economic Opportunity Act of 1964.
    c. The Comprehensive Child Development Bill.
    d. The National Institute of Education.

2. A preschool program for physically handicapped children is probably primarily

   a. Remediative.
   b. Enriching.
   c. Compensatory.
   d. Interventive.

3. A nursery school program for preschool children in a well-to-do suburb, in which the average level of education of parents is college graduate, probably primarily provides

   a. Remediation.
   b. Enrichment.
   c. Custodial care.
   d. Compensation.

4. A day care center in which children are kept clean and safe while their parents are away, but which does not have a planned play and educational program, is probably primarily

   a. Enriching.
   b. Preventive.
   c. Custodial.
   d. Interventive.

5. A day care center in which essentially normal children are not only kept clean and safe, but which also has a planned play and educational program, is probably primarily

   a. Remediative.
   b. Interventive.
   c. Custodial.
   d. Supplementary.

6. Johnny has received a baby mobile for Christmas, which includes large multicolored discs and bells and chimes which clank when the mobile is moved. Johnny will receive the most positive benefits from this if

   a. It is put away and he never sees it at all.
   b. It is suspended from his crib so he can experience it whenever he is there.
   c. It is set up by his mother when she can be near him and observe his reactions to it.
   d. It is given to his three-year-old sister to keep her from being jealous of him.

7. According to Bloom, by the time a child is age four, he has developed

   a. All of his intelligence.
   b. Approximately one-fourth of his intelligence.
   c. Approximately one-half of his intelligence.
   d. None of the above.

Section 2 *Early Intervention*

8. Hess and Shipman are known for their research on
   a. The relationship of early deprivation to later emotional problems.
   b. The relationship of maternal "teaching styles" to children's cognitive development.
   c. The relationship of compensatory programs to school achievement.
   d. The relationship of father absence to cognitive development.

9. Which of the following is not characteristic of parent-child interaction which facilitates cognitive development?
   a. When he accomplishes a new task, the child is praised.
   b. When the child speaks, the parent responds.
   c. When the child speaks, he is ignored.
   d. When the child makes a mistake, he is gently shown the correct way.

10. Johnny is old enough to walk or toddle but prefers to loll quietly in his crib or playpen. He does not maintain visual contact with his environment but usually gazes vaguely into space or hangs his head. His mealtimes are irregular and often a meal is missed. When he is fed, the menu usually consists of soft drinks, sugar-coated cereals, potato chips, and processed food. Which of the following statements does not apply to Johnny?
    a. Johnny is rapidly learning about himself and the world.
    b. Johnny is probably not well nourished.
    c. Johnny's listlessness may be due to poor nutrition.
    d. Johnny's listlessness is preventing him from interacting with his environment.

11. Which of the following statements is not true regarding the effects of nutrition on development?
    a. A poorly nourished expectant mother may not sufficiently nourish her fetus.
    b. If a population has been poorly nourished over generations, it is difficult to assess the role heredity plays in its members' intellectual development.
    c. Poor nutrition has a negative effect on the central nervous system.
    d. Nutritional level bears no relationship to cognitive development.

unit 4 models of early intervention programs

OBJECTIVES

After studying this unit, the student should be able to

- Discuss the significance of timing in early intervention programs.
- Describe the difference between parent and home-centered and child-centered group interventive models for infants, toddlers, and preschoolers.
- Describe program characteristics of representative interventive programs for various age groups.

The time at which interventive programs are introduced is an important factor in their effectiveness. When interventive programs were initiated, it was felt that they should be geared towards the traditional preschool years (ages three to five). Supposedly this would be sufficiently effective in preparing children to deal with the learning challenges of elementary school. As the programs were evaluated in terms of their ability to actually exert a sustained influence on later school performance, it seemed that apparently many were not achieving the long term results which originally had been hoped for and anticipated.

EMPHASIS ON EARLY INTERVENTION

As a result of these evaluations, a new issue was raised. Perhaps the programs were simply not intervening sufficiently early in the child's development. For example, by the time a child reached age three, his course of development might be well established, thus making substantial alteration through intervention less likely. Therefore, a movement to extend interventive programming down the age scale was undertaken. If interventive action could be provided much earlier, perhaps the results would be more generally effective and long lasting.

Today there is a variety of interventive programs which not only span the early childhood age range of birth through age five but also attempt to reach parents before their children are born so that they will learn how to provide sound developmental care for their children-to-be. There are two basic forms of interventive models: parent- and home-centered models and child-centered models. Parent- and home-centered models focus on helping parents to help their own children's development; child-centered models focus interventive efforts primarily on the children themselves.

PARENT- AND HOME-CENTERED MODELS

Those models which provide intervention by educating prospective parents in child development principles and child care practices might be subsumed under the heading, "Education for Parenthood."[1] This term is actually the name of one large scale program which has been carried out on a national basis by the Office of Child Development and the Office of Education.

Education for Parenthood

The rationale of the "Education for Parenthood" program is based on the observation that children already in school seemed to be lacking the qualities which might have

[1] Rosoff, S., Marland, S., and Kruger, W. "Education for Parenthood." *Children Today.* 2(2), 1973, pp. 3-7.

been provided for them through good parental care. Apparently their mothers and fathers lacked knowledge of both the physical and psychological needs of young children. As a result, it was suggested that a program be developed which would provide instructions in "parenting." This involves the particular skills and understanding necessary for those who have a primary responsibility for the raising of children to promote effectively the development of children. If a program such as this could reach young people before they actually became parents, they might have a greater chance of being effective with their children.

It was recognized that in a modern complex society in which institutions share so many child rearing responsibilities, families might not be teaching their children how to raise future generations. Therefore, it was felt that schools should be the community institution to assume this crucial educational responsibility. Such instruction, geared to teenagers at a time when they are making career choices, might also encourage some to consider a professional career in child care.

"Education for Parenthood" programs are now available in hundreds of high schools and reach thousands of youngsters. Curriculum content includes prenatal and biological factors in child development, infant care, basic child development, and creative activities. Many programs also provide direct contact and supervised practice with young children, often through a laboratory school. If the concept of early timing in intervention is valid, "education for parenthood" programs hold particular interventive potential. These programs indeed "intervene" at the earliest possible time — before a child is even born.

Prenatal and Postnatal Care and Education

The importance of proper prenatal and postnatal health care and education for identified prospective mothers is becoming increasingly recognized. They are seen as factors which will have later influence on the general well-being of the infants and on their potential for positive development. Health care and prenatal education therefore fall in the category of parent-centered intervention. The type of medical care an expectant mother receives for her overall health and nutrition, the biological aspects of pregnancy and the quality of psychological support she receives for her upcoming prenatal role are all related to the way in which she will view and care for her infant.

An increasing number of multifaceted early intervention programs for older children are coming to include health and education components which are targeted towards improving the functioning of the families served as a total group. In this way, the youngest children and mothers who are pregnant also benefit. Many of these programs place particular stress on nutrition education. The quality of nutrition for prospective mothers as well as for children bears a close relationship to children's cognitive and physical development. Positive nutrition is an extremely important interventive factor. Programs which increase mothers' awareness of and access to nutritionally sound foods help to provide it.

Psychological support for expectant and new parents is often given through parent education programs. The traditional methods of parent group education, discussed in more depth later, are employed. These offer parents the opportunity not only to gain concrete biological information concerning the development and care of the pregnant mother and new baby, but also to share concerns about what it means emotionally to be a parent and to consider the impact of an infant on the existing family unit. These programs also serve a preventive and interventive function, helping prospective and new parents to undertake their experience in a positive fashion.

Programs for Pregnant Unmarried Mothers

A special type of interventive model seen more in recent years is one which is designed to help pregnant unmarried women preserve developmental opportunities for both themselves and their children. An identified need if these mothers are teenagers is for accurate health information. They are often found to be particularly lacking necessary factual knowledge. They also need support in making sometimes painful decisions about the care of their baby after birth, for continued educational opportunity, and for a normal future life without stigma. Recent innovative programs have been established to meet these needs by providing quality infant group care for unmarried teenage mothers. The young mothers continue their high school education while their babies are cared for right in the educational setting. The mothers can actually spend time with their infants within the school day.

Parent- and Home-Centered Programs for Infants and Toddlers

Interventive programs for infants focus around two models. One includes those programs which encourage mothers to interact with and stimulate their infants more effectively. The other includes those which provide carefully planned group care for infants outside the home, often in settings to which the parents themselves come to participate in the activities offered.

Examples of the former model are frequently referred to as *infant stimulation* programs. Their primary interventive rationale is to increase the intellectual potential of the child. One pioneering program of this type is Dr. Ira Gordon's "Early Child Stimulation Through Parent Education" program. In order to strengthen the tie between infants and their mothers, this program employed *indigenous* (persons from the same socioeconomic background) parent educators to make home visits to help the mothers learn how to care for and stimulate their infants. Rather than working directly with the child, the visitor works with mother and child together. The visitor not only demonstrates materials and ways of providing stimulation, but also tries to help the mother develop a more positive feeling about herself and her ability to provide a positive environment for her child.

Similar programs have been established, such as Earl Schaefer's *home tutoring* program in which home visitors work with inner city families with children under two. The tutors attempt to increase parental ability to help their youngsters' development by forming relationships with the parents and children and by providing verbal stimulation and other experiences for the children.

Several parent- and home-centered program models for children from two to five are also under way. In an attempt to intervene before the child is three, the usual age of preschool entrance, there is the "Mother-Child Home Program" conducted for two-year-olds in Freeport, New York by Phyllis Levenstein. In this program, intervention to disadvantaged children is provided by "verbal stimulation" activities designed to increase the child's level of cognitive function. Components of the program include "toy demonstrators" who work with mothers and children in the home, using *verbal interaction stimulus materials.* These are various toys and books selected for their stimulating qualities.

Most parent- and home-centered programs are geared towards children under three. "Project Home Start," an alternate model of the well known group-centered Head Start program, however, is a program for three to five-year-olds which is closer to the parent-home-centered structure. This program has given parents special support in those activities which promote not only the development of preschool age children, but also of the entire family. It includes a strong nutrition component, the provision of health and social services, and home visits. All of these are intended to help reinforce the basic philosophy that parents themselves are the major facilitators of their children's development.

"Parent-Child Centers" are another kind of federally funded programs which represent a downward extension of the interventive concepts of the Head Start program. They are oriented to an earlier stage of development. The rationale of these programs is to give help to parents in their child rearing tasks and to provide direct services to the infants and toddlers themselves. The organization of these services varies from community to community. They have, however, usually included both activity in the home and development of centers to which parents and children can go for stimulating activities for the children and workshops and discussions for the parents. As with other similar programs, this one included a means of helping parents obtain proper health and psychological care.

The television program, "Sesame Street" should be mentioned an another form of home-based intervention. This program was designed to provide disadvantaged children with wider exposure to the community, to general information, and to content which would encourage the development of basic educational skills such as classifying, and counting. There has been both praise and criticism for this program. Many have a positive view of tis basic rationale, its selection of a cast to whom disadvantaged children can relate, and its ability to attract children's interest. Others have criticized it. One criticism is that it has an overstimulating format. Another is its assumption that a television program which provides only passive learning opportunity can truly have a substantial impact on developing cognitive skills at a time when children learn through active involvement. Many more feel that "Sesame Street" and similar programs are best viewed as supportive to more encompassing educational and socially oriented programming for children.

CHILD-CENTERED GROUP MODELS FOR INFANTS, TODDLERS, AND PRESCHOOLERS

Group care programs for children may have a primarily custodial or an interventive function. The intervention function means that the program not only provides adequate physical care in a safe environment, but also provides activities designed to exert a positive influence upon the child's emotional and intellectual development.

Infant and Toddler Group Care

Group care programs for infants and toddlers, either custodial or interventive, are comparative newcomers to the child care scene. A well known example of an interventive group care program is the Frank Porter Graham Child Development Center at Chapel Hill, North Carolina. The program is designed to directly intervene in the development of disadvantaged children. Means of doing this include providing stimulation and enrichment activities, such as carefully selected toys, in a child-centered environment and giving individualized care to the infants and toddlers. An interesting aspect of this program is its family style grouping with children ranging from infancy to kindergarten age in the same group. This association of children of different ages is expected to inject an additional component of stimulation.

The model of early intervention which has encompassed the largest numbers of individual programs is that which is oriented towards providing group settings for children of traditional preschool age, three to five. The prototype of such models is the well known "Project Head Start." Head Start programs have been established as half day programs as was the traditional nursery school, as summer programs prior to fall school entrance, and as all day programs. The purpose of the all day program is to provide educational and developmental experiences within a day care context.

Like most other federally funded intervention programs, Head Start also included the provision of support to parents. This has been in the form of health care services and parent involvement in program design and conduct. Head Start is widely recognized as having "put preschool education on the map."[2] It has opened the eyes of many to the need of thousands of children for interventive services.

As the Head Start program continued to evolve after its summer 1965 inception, however, increasing concern developed around its curriculum. The question was raised as to what would most effectively encourage the development of both the cognitive and socialization skills which were among the program's major objectives. Concern deepened to controversy as differing evidence as to the long term effectiveness of Head Start programs was gathered.

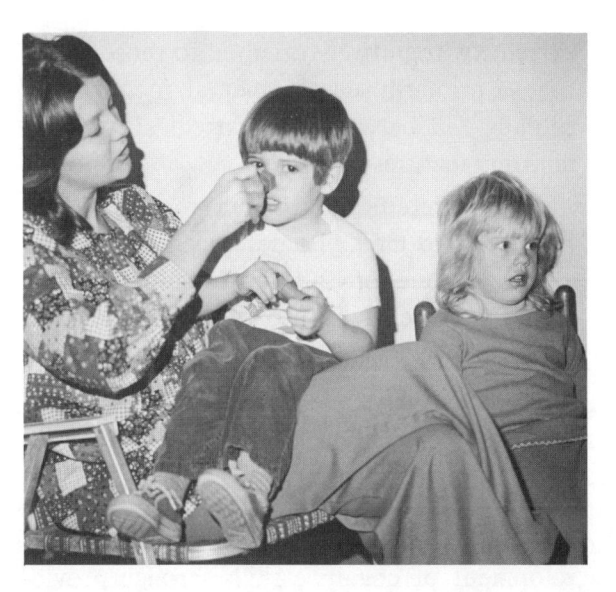

[2]M. Pines, *Revolution in Learning.* New York: Harper and Row, p. 23.

The result was the division of some preschool educators into diverse "camps" according to the type of curricular content and focus they favored. On one extreme were those who felt that free play, the staple of traditional nursery schools for middle class children, was also the most effective way of achieving both social and cognitive goals.

On the other extreme were those who felt that the play-based curriculum would not have sufficient impact on disadvantaged children, particularly in the cognitive realm. These persons thought that the curriculum should consist of academic-type experiences which would include direct instruction in skills directly related to elementary school learning tasks. These tasks would include number concepts, letter and word recognition, general information, language usage, similarities and differences between objects, and similar cognitively oriented material.

Thus, a variety of curriculum models were initiated as part of an effort to discover the *facilitating curriculum* — the means which would lead to the greatest possibility of children achieving in an academic way in elementary school.

An examination of these different models indicates that they range in content from the extremely cognitively oriented to those which have a primarily developmental focus. Most actually fall between the extremes by incorporating features of both.

The Bereiter-Engelmann model named after the two men who developed and carried it out, is one of the most widely known programs which falls into the cognitively oriented category. This curriculum is geared towards instruction in specific academic skills, such as language and word and number manipulation. Teaching strategies include direct instruction.

Two models are oriented towards the development of cognitive skills through providing children with an opportunity for direct interaction with a planned environment rather than direct instruction: (1) "The Cognitively Oriented Curriculum" of David Weikart and colleagues and (2) the Montessori method. The latter is the contemporary revival of the philosophy and methodology developed in late 19th century Italy for slum children by Dr. Maria Montessori. Weikart's curriculum, based on the theories of mental growth posed by the Swiss psychologist Piaget, is designed to assist children in experiencing some of the processes Piaget feels are the foundation of cognitive growth. In addition, stress is made on the learning benefit of play. The Montessori method also employs a more self-directed "discovery" teaching strategy. Children are exposed to increasingly complex tasks as they are ready. These models illustrate those which seem to fall in the large middle area between the two extremes of the curriculum "camps."

The developmentally based models are those which are probably the most similar to the traditional preschool play programs. Yet these approaches have become more systematic as the curriculum controversy has encouraged them to seek a more articulated theoretical rationale. For example, the traditional free play programs discouraged the planning of play experiences by teachers and, most particularly, their intervention in or structuring of ongoing play of the children. Many play-based contemporary programs involve specific efforts of teachers to encourage, guide, and facilitate play so that children profit from both its social and cognitive aspects.

A number of developmental specialists regard sociodramatic play as a means of bridging the gaps between the academically and developmentally based models. *Sociodramatic play,* as described by Dr. Sara Smilansky,[3] is a high level form of play among preschool age children. It includes the elements of basic dramatic play, in which a child imitates others and recreates situations in play through role play and make believe — "pretending," as it were. When there is verbal exchange between more than one player and they orient their dramatic play around a specific theme over a period of time, the play is sociodramatic. For example, three children may undertake to play "post office." They may incorporate materials from around the room to make a post office, mailbox, and letters. The form of their conversation might be, "Let's pretend that this is the post office. I'll be the postman. You be a clerk. You come and mail a letter." If this theme continues to develop

[3] S. Smilansky, *The Effects of Sociodramatic Play on Disadvantaged Preschool Children.* New York: John Wiley 1968, pp. 7-10.

and is "played out" for at least ten minutes, with continued interaction among the players, it is considered sociodramatic play.

Dr. Smilansky's pioneering research on disadvantaged Israeli children indicated that these children did not have the skills necessary for school success. As preschoolers, they did not have the ability to play sociodramatically. The research further suggested that for later school success, a guided form of teaching and environmental planning in preschools which would help children learn to play sociodramatically would serve to provide them with the opportunity to develop these essential skills. A careful scrutiny of the elements of this play has shown that experiencing it provides both a variety of social skills and general understanding of the world, as well as a rich base of cognitive skills, including abstraction and problem solving.

Presently, the preschool field is experiencing an increased trend back towards the play-based curriculum, oriented toward increasing the children's ability to play sociodramatically. There is growing substantive evidence of the suitability of play as an effective curricular tool in the preschool to promote both social and cognitive goals.[4]

SUMMARY

Early intervention programs are designed to increase the social and cognitive competence of children. The effort begins before the child is conceived and extends to the time he enters school. Interventive program models are either home- and parent-centered or child-centered. The latter focus direct efforts on the children themselves, while providing supplementary services for parents. The former are directly geared towards improving the functioning of parents so that they themselves can better facilitate their children's growth.

Among the specific models of early intervention programs are education for parenthood, prenatal and postnatal care and education, infant and toddler stimulation and group care, and preschool and day care programs with interventive components. There is a variety of curriculum models in early intervention programs, with varying degrees of academic and developmental focus. Increasing attention is being given to sociodramatic play as an effective curricular tool in interventive preschool programs.

SUGGESTED ACTIVITIES

- Visit several Head Start centers in your community. Observe the curricula and discuss the program philosophies with the directors or head teachers. What category of curriculum do you think each program falls into? What do you feel about its effectiveness for disadvantaged children?

- Visit several interventive programs, if possible. Observe the "teaching style" of the adults (i.e., their general approach to the children in terms of presenting activities, handling behavior, etc.). What do you think the effects of different teaching styles are on the children's learning?

- Plan to accompany a home visitor who is part of an intervention program on a visit, if possible. What approach does the visitor take with the family? Does he or she focus more on the child or on the parent?

[4] N.E. Curry, "Current Issues in Play: Theoretical and Practical Considerations for its Use as a Curricular Tool in the Preschool." Division of Instructional Experimentation, University of Pittsburgh, 1972.

- Interview several teenagers, discussing with them their attitudes toward parenthood and their conception of parental influences on child development. If any of them have participated in "Education for Parenthood" courses, ask their opinions about the value of the experience.
- Observe children at play. Watch for episodes of sociodramatic play. What do these show in terms of social and cognitive skills encouraged?

REVIEW

A. Define each of the following terms.

 Family style grouping Bereiter-Engelmann approach

 Education for parenthood Cognitively oriented curriculum

 Infant stimulation Sociodramatic play

B. Name, compare, and contrast two basic models of early intervention programs.

C. Name and define three different types of curriculum content found in preschool intervention programs.

D. Indicate the best choice for each of the following.

1. Although many health factors have been found to be important in relationship to cognitive development, one which is particularly significant is

    a. Dental condition. c. Nutrition.
    b. Care of hair and skin. d. Exposure to fresh air.

2. "Project Home Start" was primarily intended for

    a. Expectant teenage parents.
    b. Unmarried mothers.
    c. Infants.
    d. Children from 3 to 5.

3. Which of the following programs was designed specifically for two-year-olds?

    a. Education for Parenthood.
    b. Parent-Child Centers.
    c. Mother-Child Home Program.
    d. Cognitively Oriented Curriculum.

4. A "discovery" teaching strategy is a primary characteristic of

    a. The Bereiter-Engelmann approach.
    b. Education for Parenthood.
    c. The Montessori method.
    d. Project Head Start.

5. Programs which focus on strengthening the mother-child bond are primarily

   a. Parent-centered interventive programs.
   b. Much too expensive to conduct.
   c. Useless in terms of making real change.
   d. Usually conducted outside the home.

6. All of the following have been cited as strengths of the program "Sesame Street" except

   a. It extends children's fund of information.
   b. It offers children exposure to minority group role models.
   c. It offers children a passive learning experience.
   d. It readily attracts children's interest.

7. Sociodramatic play is considered to be

   a. Inadequate in facilitating cognitive development.
   b. A basis for a curriculum which can achieve both social and cognitive goals.
   c. Apt to be displayed by disadvantaged children without guidance.
   d. Most effective when teachers just observe it.

Section 3 Substitute Child Care

unit 5 child care and the changing society

OBJECTIVES

After studying this unit, the student should be able to

- State the differences between intervention and substitute child care.
- Explain the relationship between societal changes and current trends in child care practices.
- Describe some of the effects of increased interest in cognitive development on child rearing practices.
- Describe the relationship between the contemporary feminist movement and interest in substitute child care.

The need for interventive programs, described in the preceding section, has been stressed by many concerned with ways of helping all children reach their potential. An increasing concern of more and more people, in addition to parents, is for a pattern of child care services to be available to all who feel they need them. There are several reasons for this increased citizen interest in more child care programs. The reasons are related to changes in present day society, particularly to the changes in the structure of family life and the roles of family members.

INTERVENTION AND SUBSTITUTE CHILD CARE

There are two major rationales for the design of current programs for providing care and services for children outside the family. One is intervention, as a specific set of activities designed to alter the course of the child's development. The other is a means to provide *substitute child care* — provision for care of children by persons other than their parents, or other immediate family members, during times when the parents are not able to do it. The primary goal of interventive programs is to produce specific changes in the child. The goal of substitute child care is to provide safe supervision and physical care while parents are absent.

These two patterns of care are actually by no means mutually exclusive, however. Many areas of overlap exist between the two. Many programs with an interventive philosophy

44

also provide substitute child care. This may be needed by parents who work or otherwise need outside-the-home assistance. Conversely, many programs whose initial purpose may be to provide needed substitute care, place a strong stress on providing "quality" care. They intend not only to meet the children's physical needs, but also to offer experiences which serve as a positive force, like an interventive program. These programs include features specifically intended to promote the children's cognitive and social skills through careful planning and encouragement of play and through other stimulating learning experiences.

THE CHANGING SOCIETY AND SUBSTITUTE CHILD CARE

There are two forces in society which exert a substantial influence on the type of child care programming which is desired. These are the early intervention movement and the changing role of women in society.

The Early Intervention Movement

One is the movement, previously described, which grew out of the recognition of the need for intervention in the lives of disadvantaged children. This created interest in the preschool years as a time at which children may be most vulnerable to the effects of either negative or positive experiences. As the needs of disadvantaged children were given more attention, parents from all segments of society began, for different reasons, to take a new look at the kinds of experiences their preschool age children were having. The effect of interventive movement went far beyond that on those children and families for whom these programs had been initially designed.

Middle class parents had traditionally been encouraged by society to be extremely self-conscious about their child rearing practices. Popular misinterpretation of the maternal deprivation studies described earlier led both professionals and parents, encouraged by the professionals, to believe that parents were solely responsible for the way their children "turned out" as their development proceeded, both emotionally and intellectually. During the 1950s, others were frequently the subject of reports relating child disturbances to their hostility and rejection. As a result of this growing practice of "blaming" parents particularly mothers, for their children's problems, parents turned to child rearing books, "experts," and other sources to provide guidance in the overwhelming challenge of successful child rearing. Parents competed with each other. They examined their own children's achievements carefully, hoping that their children would at least hold their own in comparison to those of friends and neighbors.

Thus, when the word became widespread that the preschool years were crucial for laying down the foundation of children's learning abilities and potentials, middle class parents, wanting cognitive benefits for their children, responded along with those whose primary concern was disadvantaged children. As a result, there was a rush for home or self-help materials which parents could use to help increase their children's learning abilities. Although "Sesame Street" may have been primarily intended for disadvantaged children, thousands of middle class children also watched it. Waiting lists developed for many preschools. The traditional nursery school program, with its free play, was no longer enough. Parents began to shop around for programs with curricula they thought would place more stress on cognitive skills. For example, the Montessori method received a tremendous revival of interest in this country as parents looked for programs they felt had the appropriate cognitive focus.

Section 3 Substitute Child Care

Critics of interventive programs for the disadvantaged have stated that these programs simply attempt to impose middle class values on the children rather than truly answering their special needs. However, studies show that this is not necessarily the case. There seems to be substantial agreement among middle and lower class parents as to the educational and social goals they want for their children. Caldwell and Elardo[1] conducted research in which they reviewed previous studies and gathered their own data. Results indicated that lower and middle income parents have very similar goals for their children. Development of behaviors such as social and communication skills and the understanding of academically related concepts are seen as desirable by both.

There is a tremendous interest today on the part of many parents from all levels of society in programs which will bring about the educational achievement of their children. Parents want their children to be exposed to experiences which help them learn and develop their full potential. Many of these parents are also much more willing today than in previous years to make their voices heard about their needs and wishes for themselves and their children. All of these factors are exerting an influence on the structuring of contemporary child care programs.

CHILD CARE AND THE CHANGING ROLES OF WOMEN

The increased national interest in stimulating development of young children through program enrichment has been accompanied by another significant social trend which has tremendous implications for child rearing practices. This is the contemporary feminist movement — called, popularly, "Women's Liberation." The movement is concerned with providing equal opportunity for women to develop their full human potential. It wants to change old patterns which restrict them to sex-stereotyped roles and occupations. Since one of women's best recognized roles is that of child bearer and child rearer, women's maternal functions have come under scrutiny as a result of growing feminist activity.

Most moderate feminists, despite misinterpretations of the movement's intent, by no means reject motherhood. They do, in fact, recognize it as a very significant part of a woman's life. They do not see being a parent as a factor that must necessarily prevent adult women from achieving equal opportunity for education, employment, and professional careers. At the same time, the growing number of women who are joining the feminist movement feel that there must be a great change in America's child rearing practices. In the past, these practices relied substantially on individual mothers to carry them out. The feminists state that many more options need

[1] B. Caldwell and R. Elardo, "Value Imposition in Early Education: Fact or Fancy." *Child Care Quarterly*, 2(1), Spring, 1973, pp. 6-13.

to be available for women. Women must have the option to choose whether to become mothers at all. If they do decide to become mothers, they should then have the chance to have others participate in the task of child raising.

Thus, a growing number of people, both women and men, who support the feminist movement are demanding a total program of substitute child care services. Such programs would relieve mothers of some of the time constraints involved in being almost the sole caretakers of children during their earliest years. In this way, opportunities for full participation in adult life would be opened to women. In addition, the curricula of such programs would avoid giving children sexually stereotyped messages about female and male behavior and expectations.

It seems that the United States, in comparison with other countries such as France, China and Russia, has greatly lagged behind in providing carefully planned and financially supported substitute child care programs. The point has been made that only in twentieth century America is parenthood considered to be a full time occupation for adult women.[2]

There are historical reasons for this. The "maternal deprivation" research was one of them. Many feel that the implications of this important research were misconstrued by the suggestion that any form of substitute child care would be damaging to young children. In actuality, the research is relevant to the care of children brought up in extreme situations, such as large, impersonal, understaffed institutions, or extremely disturbed and disorganized families. It can not be generally applied to the situation where children are cared for in essentially stable nuclear families.

Other writings of the times concerned mothers. Philip Wylie wrote about "moms" — overbearing women who kept their children dependent and tied to them long past the time they should have been on their own. Edward Strecker described in *Their Mother's Sons* young men who were not able to participate in military duties because of unbreakable maternal ties. Lundberg and Farnham, in *The Lost Sex,* ascribed many societal ills to the fact that women were denying their femininity. These authors included the recommendation that women be encouraged to return to the home, rather than seek affirmation in "masculine" pursuits.

These viewpoints were representative of a strong conviction that women were not devoting sufficient time to nor displaying adequate commitment to the raising of children. Therefore, great resistance was mounted by both professionals and the parents themselves to the suggestion of substitute child care. Such programs, it was felt, should only be for children and families with special problems; poverty-level families, multihandicapped families, families where both parents had to work. It was also felt that mothers who worked or had other compelling interests might emotionally deprive their children and cause them psychological harm.

Contemporary feminists, and many child development specialists as well, take exception to these opinions. They feel that the works and opinions which supposedly support the premise that mothers should make child rearing their sole occupation, actually provide strong evidence for an opposite point of view. They see sound child development best facilitated by mothers who have outside interests in addition to the rearing of their children. Through active involvement in pursuits other than domestic activity and child care, mothers can develop a stronger sense of self and, therefore, not need to gain their total emotional gratification through the achievements of their children, or through

---

[2] Alice S. Rossi, "Equality Between the Sexes: An Immodest Proposal." *Daedalus,* Spring, 1964, pp. 607-652.

discouraging their independence. Thus, a mother having outside interests could actually prevent the "momism" which was offered as evidence that mothers should be primarily home- and child-centered until their children reached adulthood. Substitute child care would provide mothers the opportunity to participate in other activities, as well as expose their children to positive relationships with other adults. It should be emphasized that moderate feminists do not believe that mothers should give up caring for children or providing close nurturing care for them in order to truly meet their needs at various stages of development.

There is additional support for the feminist view of appropriate timing for the mother-child relationship. One fact is that modern technology and the longer life span simply do not make it necessary for women to spend their entire adult lives in child rearing and homemaking. Also, the reality of the population explosion and diminishing world resources make it crucial for women to limit family size and consider additional adult occupations.

Results of research on working mothers indicate that negative relationships between working and their children's emotional well-being have not been demonstrated. The fact of working, in and of itself, has not been shown to be correlated with incidence of emotional problems or other disturbances in children. There are many today who believe that the mother who feels a need for outside commitments or a career is so much happier that she exerts a positive influence on her children's development. She may be more stimulating company, more patient, and more attentive to her children when she is with them.

Providing models of substitute child care which permit greater sharing of child care responsibilities and allow mothers to participate more in activities outside the home also serves to reduce the isolation which many young mothers claim is their experience when their children are small. Child caring in itself is not found restrictive by most young mothers. Rather it is the fact that it must be carried out in isolation – that the mother is alone with small children all day in a house or apartment. This problem is compounded by the fact that in this country, children are not included in many settings and activities in which adults take part. There is a great child-adult segregation which may not be emotionally healthy for either. New patterns of child care might serve to reduce this separation with both adults and children feeling happier and more fulfilled.

A growing number of feminists and mothers are joining forces with parents of disadvantaged children. They are insisting that society provide a comprehensive pattern of quality substitute child care with timing and services which meet the particular needs of each and every family. Thus, comprehensive substitute child care would be built around the principles which underlie the structuring of interventive programs.

Feminists feel also that child care activities should be particularly supportive to values which are relevant to their concerns with education for sex-role development. They would like to see that nonsexist education be an integral part of any child care program in which their children participate. Essentially, this means that any kind of encouragement, overt or subtle, of sex role stereotyping be avoided. There should be nothing in the curriculum to "teach" girls that the only goals for them in life are to be wives, mothers, housewives, or members of traditional female professions such as nursing. Girls should be encouraged to play actively, rather than to be "ladylike," and would be free to take part in woodworking and other "masculine" activities.

Boys too, would be exposed to other adult role possibilities than the traditionally male jobs. Fatherhood and caring for the young would be presented in a positive light as perfectly appropriate activities for males. Boys would be encouraged to find satisfaction in housekeeping play as well as in large muscle play and block building. Both "male" and "female" props would be provided. Other educational materials would be representative of the entire spectrum of human interest. For example, books would portray both sexes engaged in a variety of activities and roles rather than those which are conventionally associated with one sex or the other.

SUMMARY

Two major features of contemporary child care are interventive programs and substitute child care programs. There are similarities and differences in these two approaches. Changing forces in society are exerting a strong influence on the press for, and structuring of, child care services. Both middle class and poverty level parents have a strong desire for educationally oriented programming which will help their children achieve in school and reach their full potential. Substitute child care and nonsexist curricula are desired by a growing number of people as a result of the feminist movement which has pointed out that there can be developmental advantages for all. The earlier resistance to substitute child care programs is breaking down as a result of these societal trends.

SUGGESTED ACTIVITIES

- Arrange to visit a day care center in your area which you have been told offers a sound developmental program. Describe those aspects of the program which meet the children's physical needs, and educational needs. How does this center represent characteristics of both substitute and interventive child care programs?
- Ask a middle class mother and a poverty level mother if they are willing to discuss with you the educational goals they hold for their children in programs in which they are participating. Compare their replies. In what ways are their goals similar or different?
- Speak with several supporters of the feminist movement about their attitudes towards parenthood, children, and child care services. Compare and contrast their opinions on the role of men in child rearing, working mothers, and the philosophy and content of child care programs.
- Ask your parents or parents from their age group what they feel societal expectations for the goals of child rearing practices were when you were a child, and from what source they feel they learned these. Compare their statements with your perception of contemporary trends and patterns in child rearing.

REVIEW

A. Define each of the following.
   1. Comprehensive child care.
   2. Quality child care.
   3. Nonsexist education.
   4. "Momism."

Section 3 Substitute Child Care

B. Compare and constrast substitute and interventive child care.
C. Describe components of a nonsexist curriculum.
D. Indicate the best choice for each of the following.
   1. Which of the following statements is not true?
      a. Working mothers do not necessarily cause emotional problems in their children.
      b. Middle and lower class parents want similar educational goals for their children.
      c. Motherhood has been a full time occupation primarily in twentieth century America.
      d. Feminists totally reject the idea of becoming mothers.
   2. Between World War II and the 1960s, which of the following was the most characteristic of child rearing practices?
      a. Mothers were strongly encouraged to work outside the home.
      b. Fathers were deeply involved in child care.
      c. Mothers frequently took their children along with them to their jobs.
      d. Mothers were the primary caretakers of young children.
   3. Nonsexist education would include all but which of the following?
      a. Boys would be encouraged to enjoy cooking.
      b. Girls would be encouraged to play quietly.
      c. Books would portray both sexes engaged in a variety of roles and activities.
      d. The housekeeping corner would contain both "masculine" and "feminine" props.

unit 6 special aspects of contemporary child rearing

OBJECTIVES

After studying this unit, the student should be able to

- Describe characteristics of contemporary trends in child rearing styles, such as single family households and group child rearing.
- Describe changes in the contemporary role of the father.
- Discuss issues involved in custody and child placement.
- Define some complex concerns in the incidence of child abuse.

The tremendous societal upheavals of the past decade have had a strong impact on child rearing. Not only have they influenced the types of services parents claim they want for themselves and their children, but also the actual styles of child rearing they practice. The most common mode of child raising today is within the traditional nuclear family unit. However, there is an increasing development of alternative styles of child rearing which were considered less acceptable and were less prevalent in earlier years. Aspects of contemporary child care are reflected also in different viewpoints of ways of handling children who must be cared for by people other than their parents. In recent years, unfortunately, child abuse seems to be increasing.

SINGLE PARENT HOUSEHOLD

In the years since 1960, there has been a significant increase in the number of households or families headed by one parent. Statistics show that there are millions of children living in households headed by either mothers or fathers. The parent of the opposite sex is not present.

Single parent families occur in all cultural and economic groups. Recent societal trends are reflected in the large number of women who are heads of households. As a result of the feminist movement, more and more women seek independence and are willing to undertake serving as the sole support for their children. The increasing divorce rate has found more women, still in most cases assuming custody of the children, becoming the heads of households. At the same time, more and more fathers have become single parents, with responsibility for the care of young children. In some cases — often widely publicized — mothers have decided to strike out on

51

their own and have left their children in the care of the father. In addition, more and more fathers are asking for and receiving custody of their children in divorce cases. There are current shifts in viewpoints on the role functions of both men and women as child rearers. Perhaps for this reason, more men are coming to feel comfortable in serving the nurturing function of a parent.

Despite the increase of single parent families, there is debate surrounding the effects of single parent status on children. Many feel that it is the personal qualities of the parent which are important. It is his or her commitment to the child and the general type of emotional climate that can be provided which has significance to the child, rather than the fact of the presence of two parents under one roof. There is a belief that a child living with one happy single parent will receive a more positive experience than the child living with two parents who are in constant conflict. Others feel that this fragmentation and lack of intimate exposure to both parental figures at the same time may lead to negative consequences. This would be particularly likely if the child and parent did not have access to quality substitute child care programs to provide other relationships for the child.

With single parenthood on the increase, many single parents are developing their own support systems to help them carry out both their adult lives and child rearing functions as soundly as possible. Some parents form neighborhood groups for discussions and other activities. Others share child care responsibilities or form telephone networks. A more formal organization of single parents called "Parents Without Partners" provides them the opportunity to meet each other, to share mutual concerns, and to develop mutually helpful projects.

GROUP CHILD REARING

Families are traditionally considered as living in a house, apartment, or other unit in which there are no persons who are not relatives. Today, however, a number of parents, both single and married, are participating in group or *communal* living and child rearing arrangements. In such arrangements, either one or both of the parents live within a larger group. The larger group is made up of other parents and children; all members of the household share in the child care and domestic activities necessary to carry out living functions. The physical setting may be a large apartment, house, or farm. Several reasons for the increase in communal living patterns have been posed. These include dissatisfaction with the isolation and intensity of nuclear family relationships, resentment of the typical "establishment" life-style, and a search for ways to combat feelings of alienation and to experience new commitments and challenges.

The actual experience of children in communal child rearing may vary from setting to setting. In many instances, the children hold a very close relationship with their parents as primary caretakers, just as they would in a one-family household. As the children become older, however, "multiple mothering" becomes increasingly introduced into the caretaking arrangements. Children in communal arrangements are also influenced by others similar in age to themselves because of their close association with the children of other parents sharing the living facilities.

With the advent of communal child rearing arrangements has come an interest in knowing whether being raised under such conditions results in a different type of adult personality. Such settings have not existed in the United States long enough or in sufficient numbers to permit the children to be studied as adults.

Studies of communal child rearing in other cultures, such as Israeli *kibbutzim,* are available. The results of such studies must be considered carefully, however. Bruno Bettelheim, in his well known and controversial book, *The Children of the Dream*,[1] suggested that children raised in the group settings of the kibbutz grew up to be emotionally healthy and capable of achievement. In fact, these children did not show either the positive or negative extremes of developmental dimensions — such as intelligence, personality depth, and emotional disturbance — which are found in children brought up primarily in nuclear families. For example, there is a wide range of intelligence in American children. Some are very slow, and others extremely bright. Kibbutz children were found to fall more in the middle ranges. There was less incidence of emotional disturbance found among communally raised children. This was among the reasons for Bettelheim's suggestion that communal patterns of child rearing could be more effective than care provided in poverty homes, or for that matter, in many middle class homes as well.

ROLE OF THE FATHER IN CHILD CARE

As was stated earlier, it is becoming increasingly recognized that fathers play a significant role in the development of their children. The interest of feminists in involving fathers more directly in child care has brought with it by-products which are beneficial to parents and children alike. The fathers themselves are encouraged to feel comfortable about assuming a caretaker role along with the more traditional one of provider. Many fathers no longer feel self-conscious about joining in the care of small children or in other domestic tasks. In some families, fathers may actually stay home and care for the house and children while the mothers work outside. In an increasing number of other families, both parents equally share the child care and provider roles. In still other families, one parent may work at home for one or more years while the other one goes out to work, and then they may reverse these roles for another period of time. These flexible "life-styles" provide each individual with greater opportunity for a variety of meaningful experiences and, hence, for greater self-fulfillment.

Among the many benefits to the children of the increased involvement of fathers in their care is the likelihood that it may help in their cognitive development. A research finding which has emerged along with the recent interest in cognitive development shows that when fathers are involved in their early care, children experience a positive influence on later cognitive development. "Father absence" during formative years has been identified as a factor with negative effects on emotional and cognitive development of both boys and girls.

Thus, one of the greatest functions of the father, or other male figure in the case of fatherless children, is in helping children learn what men are like. Some observers have

[1] B. Bettelheim, *The Children of the Dream*. New York: MacMillan, 1969.

noted that fathers relate to children — and give children the opportunity to relate back — in a variety of ways.[2] Mothers are more apt to be consistent in their approach. Fathers play an important role also in helping children constructively separate from their mothers. They help bridge the transition from the mother to the "wider world."

The significance of the father's role in development is not counter to the feminist's wish for equality of opportunity for both sexes. The fact that each sex offers special qualities to contribute to the growth of the child does not mean that rigid sex role stereotyping is taking place. Rather, it indicates that basic differences are acknowledged in the process of becoming human which is the major task of all children.

PLACEMENT AND CUSTODY OF CHILDREN

There have always been children whose parents, for various reasons, have not been able to care for them. Society in these cases has had to provide other forms of care. Recent trends in child rearing are exerting an influence on ways in which children are handled in the absence or incapacity of their own parents. *Placement* — the term for the arrangements which may have to be made for such children — refers to the processes involved in such actions as adoption, foster care, and awarding of custody in divorce. Old procedures and constraints in placement practices are shifting. One area in which this is taking place is in adoption. *Adoption* is a legal transaction which gives the child all the rights of a natural child of the parents. The parents have the same legal responsibilities to the child as if he were their own. *Foster parents* are persons who take on parental duties of providing home care for children during a period of time when they require total substitute care. They do not legally adopt the child.

Adoption "matching" procedures are less rigid today. Formerly, for example, to adopt a child, a family not only had to represent the traditional "nuclear" structure, but also had to match the prospective child's race, religion, and general social and intellectual background. Usually, the adoptive mother was not permitted to work outside the home. More recently, these practices have changed. Perhaps this is due in part to the growing illegitimacy rate, as well as to social pressures for greater acceptance of different styles of living. Adoption policies have definitely become more liberal. Today, adoptions by single parents and interracial couples take place. Some adoption agencies indicate that handicapped children who are difficult to place find homes with single adoptive parents.

Changes are also occurring in custody decisions in divorce cases. Children are no longer almost automatically placed with the mother. In more and more instances, the father may receive custody.

In all cases of child placement, however, increasing emphasis on the rights of the children themselves is contributing towards some substantial changes in the procedures involved. Guidelines are being followed in practices which will promote the optimal development of the children. Their need for continuity of relationships is given priority over the legal prerogative of adults.

Many key developmental questions related to the design of interventive and substitute care programs have been raised around adoption and other placement activities: What is the effect on emotional development of separation from a prime caretaker, particularly at an early age? What is the need of children for continuous contact with a primary caretaker?

---

[2] J. Dreiss, "The Psychological Effects of Fathering, or What Are Daddies For" *Pittsburgh Area Preschool Association Publication,* 1974.

A recent book, *Beyond the Best Interests of the Child*,[3] is concerned with the issues involved in meeting the child's needs in placement procedures. Every child, it states, has a crucial need for a "psychological parent" with whom he can sustain a long term, consistent relationship. Placement practices have not respected these needs and must be altered if "the best interests of the child" are to be met.

Several types of changes should be made to meet placement needs. Foster children who have been with one set of foster parents during their formative years should not be returned later to the biological parents, despite their legal prerogatives. In all likelihood, the child feels the foster parents to be his psychological parents. It would be extremely disruptive to the child to break these ties. In the same vein, probationary periods for future adoptive parents are not indicated. This would create a time of instability and unpredictability in the relationship at the time the child needs closeness and continuity. The suggestion is also made that in divorce cases there should be no court order visits to the parent who is not awarded custody. Divided loyalty and conflict in the child can result from this practice. If carried out, the change would pose a hardship to divorcing couples, however. Both might be highly adequate and committed in the role of parent; one would inevitably and undeservingly be denied contact with the child.

It can be said that this refined scrutiny of the many complex issues in contemporary child placement should indeed help to "humanize" the impersonal procedures which have been harmful and disruptive to children. At the same time, it also points up that there are many profound dilemmas in the child care field which need to be resolved before the welfare of all human beings is achieved.

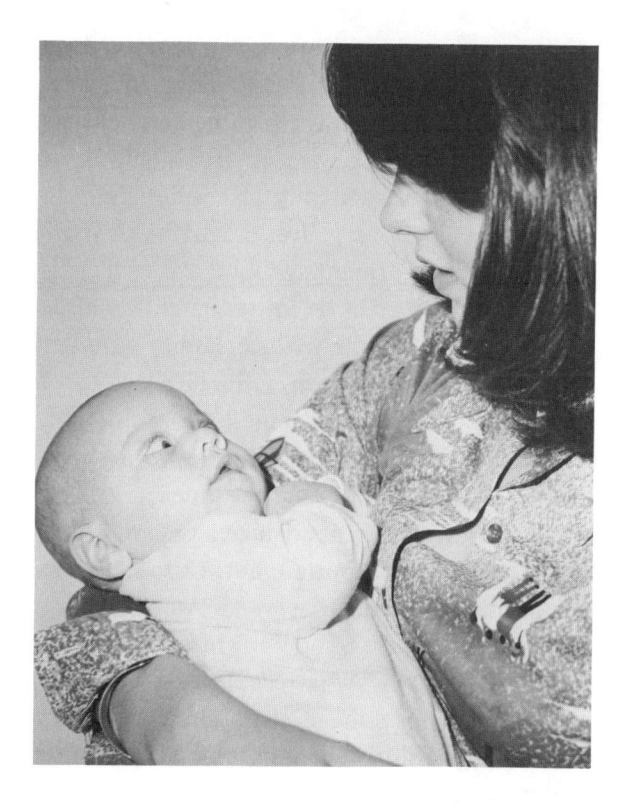

[3] J. Goldstein, A. Freud, and A. Solnit. *Beyond the Best Interests of the Child.* New York: The Free Press, 1973.

CHILD ABUSE

One of the unresolved dilemmas in child care is posed around the incidence of child abuse, or *the battered child syndrome* as it has also been called. This unfortunate practice can involve neglect as well as physical abuse. It is either becoming more prevalent or seems to be as increased evidence of its occurrence surfaces.

Child abuse is found to occur in families in all socioeconomic levels. It seems to happen most frequently among parents who have married young. Abusive families are frequently discovered when they bring children to hospitals. Parents may claim the children's injuries were received accidentally. Certain injuries may cause medical personnel to suspect that in actuality they were inflicted intentionally. Sometimes suspected abuse cases are reported by concerned neighbors or others involved with the child.

A search for ways to prevent child abuse and to understand the context in which it occurs continues. The complexities involved in dealing with it are becoming readily apparent. On one hand, vulnerable and helpless children living in abusive environments must be protected for their physical well-being. In some cases their very lives might be in jeopardy. Certainly, their psychological welfare is at stake as well. On the other hand, it can be difficult to determine with certainty whether a family indeed has been deliberately abusive or whether the injuries might be accidental.

Recent child abuse legislation has been enacted which may require physicians and others believing they recognize a case of abuse to report it to appropriate authorities. There is considerable controversy, however, as to the most effective mode of intervention in such instances: In what cases does "corporal punishment" become abuse? In what cases should the child be removed from the parents? Under what circumstances, if any, should legal proceedings and penalties be instituted against parents? What happens in a case of mistakenly "diagnosing" a case of abuse? These are some of the issues which confront those exposed to child abuse situations.

One line of thought suggests the consideration of the types of parents who are abusive and the relationship of the parents' own personal backgrounds to the abusive behavior. Frequently, it has been found, abusive parents are people who were severely deprived and neglected as children. In fact, they may have been abused themselves. As adults, it is difficult for them to meet the dependency needs of others when their own have never been met. They may expect their children to actually "parent" them. When the children naturally cannot do this, the parents become furious.

Some abusive parents, in addition, live under circumstances which would be difficult for anyone to tolerate: financial problems, general family disorganization, and isolation. Many are made unequal to the physical demands of parenthood by fatigue and poor health. All these factors detract further from their ability to provide nurturing care to their children. Often abusive parents are ignorant in terms of developmental expectations for children. When their children cannot behave at a level in line with these inappropriate expectations, the parent may become enraged and abusive.

A parent support system which would help parents improve their own lives in order to better meet the demands of child rearing would be one step toward breaking the abusive chain. Increased access to substitute child care, health and counseling services, educational and employment opportunities, and provision for financial stability would be components of such programs. Some areas have recently developed "day care" for abused infants and toddlers. By providing separation and supportive services for parents, they intervene in the abusive situation.

Some abusive parents have formed discussion groups, such as "Parents Anonymous," and "hot line" systems. When they feel they are about to be abusive, they can make contact with others who have had similar experiences and can help them in controlling their abusive urges.

The causes of child abuse are probably best addressed at their source — the deficiencies in the total societal pattern of child care — rather than by patchwork efforts after the abuse has taken place. Thus, intervention and prevention, rather than punishment, would ultimately be the most positive approaches.

SUMMARY

Rapid social changes are exerting an influence on traditional modes of child rearing and causing various problems related to child care to come to public attention. The number of single parent households is increasing; either the mother or the father may be head of the family. Some young parents are living in group, or communal, settings in which other adults participate in the activities necessary for living and child rearing. A positive advance in contemporary child rearing practices is the greater involvement of many fathers in child rearing. Father participation has been related to positive sex role and cognitive development.

"Placement" guidelines for children who are undergoing adoption, foster care, or divorce custody proceedings are needed which recognize and respect the child's need for a "psychological" parent. Child abuse is a growing phenomenon which probably requires a preventive and supportive approach to resolve some of the complex issues surrounding it.

SUGGESTED ACTIVITIES

- If there is one in your area, see if you can arrange to visit a commune. What seems to be the philosophy of child rearing there? What differences do you see between this and your perception of that which governs nuclear families raising children?

- Find out about your community's "Parents Without Partners" organization. What kinds of program and supports do they offer to single parents?

- Visit a social agency which handles child placements. Find out about its guidelines regarding adoption and foster care. Ask if these are essentially the same (or different) as they were ten years ago.

- If you are acquainted with a pediatrician, ask the doctor's opinion of the child abuse legislation in your state. Explain the reason for your interest as a student of child development and child care.

- Contact the Center for Prevention of Child Abuse, or similar program, in your area. What kinds of services do they provide? What is the rationale for these services?

- Observe a father and a mother with their son and daughter. Are there any differences in the way the parent of each sex relates to his/her children of the opposite sex? What is the general "style" of each parent? Is it the same or different with the opposite sex child? Do these parents fit the general conception of fathers being somewhat more strict and mothers somewhat more nurturant?

- Interview several different fathers. What "parenting" roles do they play? How do these compare with the descriptions of father roles in the text?

REVIEW

A. Define each of the following.

1. Parents Without Partners
2. Communal child care
3. Battered child syndrome
4. Psychological parent

Section 3 Substitute Child Care

B. Indicate the best choice for each of the following.

1. Which of the following is not true?

    a. Single people are often permitted to adopt children today.
    b. Fathers are becoming increasingly involved in child care.
    c. Extremes of intelligence and personality characteristics have not been displayed by communally raised adolescents.
    d. Child abuse is found only among poverty level families.

2. Which of the following has not contributed to the increase of single parent families?

    a. Increasing divorce rate.
    b. Population explosion.
    c. Increasing interest by fathers in child rearing.
    d. Influence of the feminist movement.

3. Which of the following is not a reason for the increase of communal living and child rearing?

    a. Disenchantment with "the establishment."
    b. Dissatisfaction with the nuclear family.
    c. Financial problems.
    d. Wish to combat feelings of alienation.

4. Which of the following is not true of the father's contribution to child development?

    a. There is no relationship between experiencing fathering and cognitive development.
    b. Fathers help children separate from their mothers.
    c. Fathers help children learn what men are like.
    d. Fathers provide children new ways of experiencing the world.

5. Incidence of child abuse is felt to be related to

    a. Parents' deprivation in their own childhoods.
    b. Parents' hobbies and interests.
    c. Parents' cultural backgrounds.
    d. Number of children in the family.

6. Which does not apply in child placement to "meet the best interests of the child:"

    a. Biological parents could not claim foster children after the child had grown close to the foster parents.
    b. Adoptions would be made permanent from the start.
    c. Biological parents could claim their children from foster parents at any time.
    d. Frequent foster placement would be harmful to the child.

unit 7 models of substitute child care

OBJECTIVES

After studying this unit, the student should be able to
- Describe current issues in substitute child care.
- Describe characteristics of infant and toddler child care programs.
- Describe characteristics of day care programs.
- List other forms of substitute child care.
- Identify issues related to the development of day care programs.

Understanding substitute child care involves more than recognizing the need for it and the different models of substitute child care programs. It also entails an awareness of some widely held attitudes which influence the form, amount, and consumers of such services.

ISSUES IN SUBSTITUTE CHILD CARE

Key issues in substitute child care are oriented to the questions of whom substitute care should be for, how much of it should be made available, and what its long term effects might be. These concerns arise because the larger society has, for many years, rejected the idea of organized substitute child care. There have been several reasons for this.

One reason is the deeply ingrained contention that mothers, if at all able, should be at home with their young children. In this way, they would provide the bases for the functioning of the family and the raising of the children. Those who hold this attitude feel that substitute child care should be available only to mothers who are living under special or unusual circumstances. For example, they feel day care would be appropriate for those who are single heads of the household and are the only source of financial support. Others believe that the constant presence of the mother in the home is so important that all mothers should be paid to stay there, rather than seek income by outside work. Still others suggest that substitute child care should be primarily for mothers in low income brackets. The reasoning is that if day care and similar programs are available to these mothers, they will be able to work and stay off the welfare rolls, or they can acquire training which will enable them to find a job which will allow them to be self-supporting.

A viewpoint which is becoming increasingly accepted is that substitute child care programs should be available to everybody, in a variety of patterns, to meet the child care needs of each particular family. This care would not simply be "custodial;" it would be of high quality. A developmentally based program for the child and a variety of supportive services to the family would be of benefit to all.

Many developmental specialists pose objection to the suggestion that substitute child care should only be targeted towards those who are disadvantaged. They would probably agree, however, that with limited resources for program support, people in poverty circumstances should have priority. They validly point out that using day care and other substitute child care to force mothers to go out and work if they actually prefer to remain home with their young children is harmful. In addition, segregation of one segment of society's children in a pattern of care different from that of the rest may contribute to communication problems and lack of understanding between the various groups as they grow into adulthood.

Comprehensive child care — the term used to denote programs offering a variety of services to the family — would not fragment the family. By helping families obtain services which would improve their functioning, such programs actually could strengthen family ties and the contribution to family life of each member. Many such programs have a component of parent involvement. Parents are not considered as simply consumers of the program. They are also participants in designing and carrying it out. Such parent involvement not only contributes to consistent care for the children, but also provides a vehicle for reduction of the isolation which is so destructive to today's family life. Frequent moving and suburban life make it difficult for many families to develop close ties with their neighbors and community support services. Many young mothers report that it is not caring for their young children which they find difficult and depressing. Rather, it is the fact that with husbands almost universally working away from the home, they find themselves left alone in the house. They have little access to other adult company and activities. Available child care services with parent participation can provide such mothers an opportunity to join with other adults while knowing that their children are receiving care.

MODELS OF SUBSTITUTE CARE

The most recent programs of substitute child care to be established are those for care of very young children. In some states, group care for children under three has been illegal and this, along with the fact that the wider acceptance of substitute care for older children has not extended downwards, had caused the development of such programs to proceed more slowly.

Programs for Infants and Toddlers

Day care homes (family day care) are the most common mode of substitute infant and toddler care. These are private homes in which small groups of children are cared for by a "family day care mother." The mother may or may not have young children of her own for whom she provides care. She may or may not receive compensation for her services. Child care licensing regulations apply to family day care homes although many are not licensed. Regulations usually limit the number of children who can be cared for to six or seven when there is one caretaker.

The rationale behind family day care or day care homes is that such home based care provides the appropriate "homelike" atmosphere which is most suitable for young children. However, *quality control* (a safeguard that the children are receiving care which is sound not only physically but also in terms of provisions for a stimulating and emotionally supportive environment) is particularly hard to achieve in family day care homes.

Many family day care mothers may indeed love children and be able to offer them individual, warm and nurturing care. However, they may lack knowledge of ways to make their home cognitively enriching by arranging it to promote appropriate exploratory and play activity. One reason for this is that family day care mothers — because their work sites are in their own homes — have the least access to programs training them specifically for their work. Another drawback of the family day care home model is that these mothers, unlike other professionals, perform their work in isolation. This is similar to the circumstances of many real mothers. They have nobody "to sit down with" at the end of a day to exchange ideas and concerns. Therefore, these mothers have little opportunity to develop a professional identity or a motivation to improve their skills through association with others. Training programs for family day care mothers have, fortunately, begun to increase during the past few years, frequently under the sponsorship of licensing agencies. These have provided a forum for bringing the day care mothers together and have increased their sense of professionalism.

Infant and Toddler Group Care is a more recent model of substitute child care for children under three. Many of these models have been initiated as pilot or demonstration projects, designed to gather data to answer the question of whether group care given outside of private homes can provide the kinds of experience these very young children need.

In these settings, a home or even a particularly homelike environment is not the prime characteristic. The focus is not necessarily on attempting to replicate a family model of care. Rather, the program structure is more parallel to that of a day care or residential setting for older children. Such programs include a daily schedule, activity and play areas, and a variety of staff members who provide both direct care and support services.

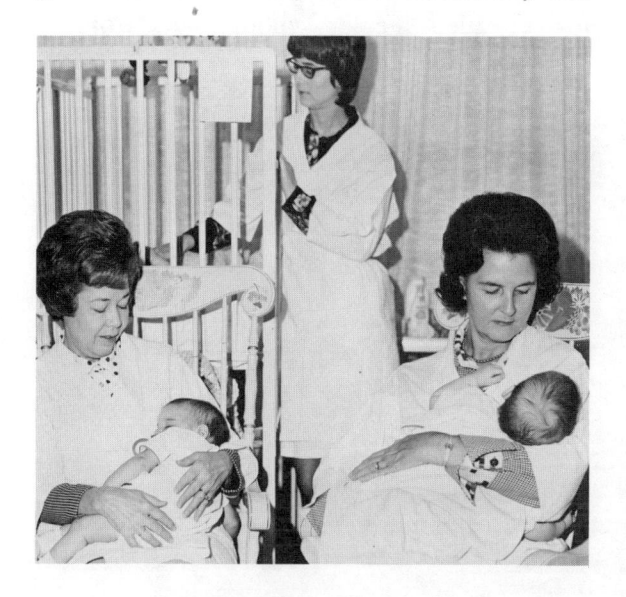

One of the best known infant-toddler group care programs is that developed by Mary Elizabeth Keister at the university of North Carolina at Greensboro. This program, which was primarily conducted in the education wing of a church building, represents an attempt to provide individualized care, stimulating surroundings, and, in general, a "quality" experience. Dr. Keister has described her staffing model as "multiple mothering."[1] Each child has contact with more than one staff member during a day, although each room has one person in charge.

The children in this center come from a variety of socioeconomic backgrounds. This is in accordance with the goal to demonstrate the possibility of providing sound developmentally based infant group care rather than specifically to provide intervention for disadvantaged children. To provide the opportunity to play is a particular feature of this program.

Evaluation studies of the effectiveness of the demonstration projects compare infants in the centers with similar infants being raised in homes. The studies seem to indicate that it is possible to create the kinds of conditions that provide quality care rather than just custodial care. No significant differences were found in various measures of social and cognitive development between the infants in Dr. Keister's center and babies cared for at home.

Results of such studies are provocative. It still has not been possible to assess the long term, adult outcomes of having been exposed to group care programs during infancy. However, it does seem as if the new models may hold potential. Perhaps, if the early evidence is borne out, quality substitute care for infants will indeed provide greater opportunity

[1] M.E. Keister, *"The Good Life" for Infants and Toddlers.* Washington: National Association for the Education of Young Children, 1970.

for some young children. These are the infants who otherwise might have been cared for in unstimulating, inconsistent, and in some cases, punitive homes.

The main concern at this point about infant and toddler substitute child care programs is that there may be a major difference in the basic quality of demonstration programs and others developed under more informal circumstances. Demonstration programs are usually conducted by experts with adequate funding for the careful execution of the program, with sufficient staff and suitable facilities. Programs established by poorly trained people with inadequate resources may well be extremely damaging to the children who are cared for in them.

Group Day Care

The best known model of substitute child care for children between three and five is group day care, or "day care," as it is commonly called. The regulations of some states do not permit group care for children under three. While some children in the three-to-five age group may be cared for in day care homes, the majority of them are in day care centers.

In many ways, day care centers are quite similar to half-day nursery school programs. Upon entering a day care center, one might encounter a classroom equipped very much in the same way as a preschool classroom. Large and small muscle play equipment would be present, along with shelves with books, blocks, art materials, and other mainstays of any developmentally based program. There would be areas for quiet and active play and child-size tables and chairs. Similarly, staff members in day care centers are usually called teachers rather than child care workers or other titles which denote all-day or residential caregivers. Much of the daily program of a day care center is like that of a regular preschool.

There are routines, such as snack time, and other periods which organize the day and differentiate time and space for the children: free play, story time, outdoors time. Perhaps music, cooking, a walk, and a field trip are provided on certain days.

The main similarity among family day care, infant group care, regular preschool programs, and day care centers is probably the concern of those supporting their use that they provide more than a custodial program. In this way, substitute child care programs have value for all children, not just those who "need" it because their parents cannot serve as full time caretakers.

A closer look shows the differences between day care centers and mursery schools. Day care centers must provide the additional resources necessary to care for children on an all-day basis. In some centers these day may be long, indeed — from an early opening time at seven in the morning to a closing time of six in the late afternoon — so that parents have time to deliver and pick up children before and after working hours. Staff hours are very different in day care centers. There must be shifts to cover the long hours that the centers are in operation. Many centers provide the greatest number of staff during what might be called regular school hours from

9 A.M. to 4 P.M. During these times when the most children are likely to be present, the most enriched programming and individual care are provided.

Many day care centers have variable attendance options for the children. Some may arrive early in the morning and leave in mid-afternoon; others may arrive later and leave later. Some children may come just for mornings; others, just for afternoons. Day care programs may have larger enrollments than nursery schools. With more children often present at the same time, day care programs may use several rooms or even an entire house or building for its program.

Day care centers must include special facilities for the physical care of children. Unlike preschools, they must be able to serve meals. Some preschools may include a meal as part of their program, but this is an optional feature. Day care centers must have food preparation and serving facilities as well as a staff to take the responsibility for meals. When young children spend the entire day in a day care center, they need a time for rest. Half-day preschool programs usually offer rugs or mats upon which the children can lie comfortably for a quiet period. In day care centers, however, more extensive arrangements must be made for the children to rest. Cots are often used so that children can nap during the day. In addition, a special area is usually set aside to serve as an infirmary for children who become sick while at the center.

Many larger day care programs employ staff in addition to the teachers, assistants, and program director. They may have a social worker who is responsibile for intake of children, preparation of social and developmental histories, and assistance to families in learning about and taking advantage of other community services. Additional housekeeping staff, such as a housekeeper and custodian, may be necessary in day care programs to adequately maintain the physical setting according to health and safety standards. A nurse may be on full or part time duty. Large day care programs must employ a full time administrator or executive director in order to effectively carry on their work. As the leader of the program, the administrator is responsible for the conduct of all aspects of it. He or she must be able to relate to the community, the parents, and the staff of the center. The administrator must also provide guidelines for the operation of the center and see that it has adequate resources available to carry out the program.

Some of the larger day care programs, particularly those receiving federal or state funding support, may also involve consultants. These persons who have special expertise in various areas help the center staff carry out an effective program. For example, a psychologist or psychiatrist may confer with the staff about ways of handling problem or puzzling behavior in the children; a nutrition consultant may work with the staff to assure that the meals are well balanced.

Day care programs are conducted or sponsored in a variety of ways. Many are funded by federal, state, and local sources, in addition to any fees participating families may pay — fees based on a "flat" rate or a sliding scale based on family income. Other centers might be established by private groups, still according to the requirements of state licensing regulations for child care centers. For example, groups of parents may organize to establish and run a day care program. They may pool their resources to reduce expenses and may share teaching duties as well as administrative responsibility in *parent cooperatives*. Day care centers have also been conducted within public school programs, serving preschool age children and providing an educational component under the total administration of the school system.

A recent development in the day care field, consonant with the societal recognition of the importance of the preschool years and the press to develop programs to provide early education, has been the opening of commercial day care centers. These centers are conducted for profit by private owners, either individuals or large businesses and companies. Many commercial centers, as is true of private centers, offer a sound, developmentally-oriented experience for the children. They provide trained staff, a flexible child-centered program, and sufficient resources. There has been some indication that some profit making programs may rely too much on a preplanned, prescribed program and fail to provide adequate staff and materials. Commercial centers may employ formal advertising techniques in order to appeal to parents. An offshoot of the profit-making centers is franchised day care, which is similar to restaurant franchises in that there is a basic plan for the centers which is duplicated in all of their locations.

There are still other types of day care centers. Community child care is a concept supported by many, including feminists. In this model, a community uses a variety of funding sources and employs its own administrative control to conduct day care. Other day care centers are conducted by industries for their female employees; others, by colleges and universities to both provide substitute care for students, faculty, and staff and as laboratory training sites as well.

Other Forms of Substitute Child Care

Private arrangements involving relatives, "baby sitters" and neighbor exchanges still comprise a substantial amount of contemporary child care. When children are in need of substitute care on an emergency basis, there are other options although these are extremely limited. Twenty-four-hour child care — providing around the clock service to parents for care at any time they may need it — is still extremely rare, although it is being increasingly demanded. Foster home care, in which a child is placed for long term care in another home, is a form of substitute child care. "Homes" or "shelters" operated by welfare departments are sources of publicly sponsored long term care.

A model of substitute child care for emergency situations which seems quite sound from both a developmental and financial point of view is *homemaker service*. Homemakers are people with domestic and child caring skills who go to a home when one or both parents are unable to assume caretaking responsibilities because of illness or some other reason. They take over the housekeeping and care of the children until the parents can resume it. Since this form of child care helps to keep the family together, sustains continuity of environment for the children, and is less expensive to provide than group homes, it holds great promise.

SUMMARY

Substitute child care is a controversial issue. There has been a strong conviction among many people that the child should be cared for at home during his preschool years. As a result of societal changes, substitute child care is now seen as having potential to solidify, rather than fragment, family life.

Substitute care for infants and toddlers is provided primarily through family day care, with new models of infant group care presently appearing. Lacks in both models include the absence of quality control for family day care homes. Infant group care demonstration programs which have been well funded may tempt those with less expertise and resources to begin similar programs.

Children from three to five may be cared for either in family day care or group day care centers. Good quality day care provides a sound developmentally based program and other important services to the children and their families. In some ways, day care centers are similar to half-day nursery schools. Day care centers require many additional resources in order to provide adequate all-day care to children, however. There is a variety of sponsorships of day care programs. Among other forms of substitute child care, the homemaker model holds promise for families in emergency situations.

SUGGESTED ACTIVITIES

- Talk with several young mothers about their attitudes towards substitute child care. How do they feel about staying home with their young children? What do they seem to like most and least about it?

- Talk to a variety of people — men, college students, grandparents, mature women — about their opinions of substitute child care. How do they feel about the availability of child care services for all? What role do they feel public funding should play in child care?

- Arrange to visit a family day care home to determine its developmental aspects. Observe the physical layout of the house, the play equipment available, and the activity program for the children. What is the agency sponsorship of the home? What supports does it offer the day care mother?

- Talk with a family day care mother about her job. How does she view the needs of the children? What does she feel are the gratifications and frustrations of her job?

- If there is a center for infant-toddler group care in your community, arrange to visit it. How does its program compare to what you think a home gives children? How does the center provide for stimulation and continuity of care?

- Visit several group day care centers. How does the educational or developmental aspect of the program of one differ from that of the other? What family support services do the centers provide?

- Visit a "franchise" or profit-making day care center. What are your impressions about the program?

- Talk with several working mothers. What are their substitute child care arrangements? How do they feel about them?

Section 3 Substitute Child Care

REVIEW

A. Define each of the following terms.

1. Family day care
2. Pilot program
3. Infant and toddler group care
4. Quality child care
5. Comprehensive child care
6. Franchise day care
7. Parent Cooperative

B. Briefly answer each of the following.

1. Compare and contrast the day care model and the nursery school models and child care programs.

2. Describe the differences between nonprofit and profit-making day care centers and the differences in models of day care sponsorship.

3. List some of the types of staff employed in a day care center.

C. Indicate the best choice for each of the following.

1. Which of the following premises is not relevant to the issue of comprehensive quality day care?

    a. Day care should be for persons on welfare so they can work and become self-supporting.
    b. Day care services are available to all as they feel the need.
    c. Day care services should provide supports to the total family.
    d. Day care includes developmental programming as well as good physical care.

2. Which of the following is the most difficult problem for young mothers staying at home to care for young children?

    a. Absence of the father during the day.
    b. Isolation from other adults.
    c. The child care itself.
    d. Having to do some housework.

3. In many states, it is illegal to have group care for children under age

    a. One.   c. Three.
    b. Two.   d. Four.

4. Which of the following would not be considered a deficiency in the family day care model?

   a. Family day care mothers may like children.
   b. Family day care mothers may have no training.
   c. Family day care mothers may not know how to provide stimulation.
   d. Family day care mothers have little contact with other family day care mothers.

5. A major concern of those assessing the quality of infant group care is that

   a. The children will not receive good physical care.
   b. The children will not be allowed to play.
   c. People will try to develop centers with insufficient resources.
   d. The program will sabotage the family.

Section 4 Parent-Teacher Contacts

unit 8 establishing parent-teacher contacts

OBJECTIVES

After studying this unit, the student should be able to

- Explain the significance of school-parent relationships for positive child development.
- Describe the relationship between parenthood and community institutions and between continuity of care and parent-teacher relationships.
- Describe dynamics of communication between parents and teachers.
- List and define structural aids to communication.

With modern industrial society have come many changes in ways of viewing and caring for children. Even though public schools were conducted in the 19th century, the major responsibility for determining the content of children's experiences and their education fell primarily on their parents. At that time, the concept of a day care center for young children did not exist. The essential care of children was given within the family unit. In recent years, this has changed. Institutions of various kinds have assumed functions which were formerly the sole province of individual families or extended families.

Today many sources external to the home help to give services to young children and families. This is not to imply, however, that families do not play a significant role in influencing the development of their children. Rather, it seems that families and societal institutions both contribute to it.

WHY SCHOOL-PARENT RELATIONSHIPS?

It is extremely important that all who share responsibility for the care and nurture of young children work together. All sources will then provide the kinds of experiences which meet the particular needs of each child.

This is the reason for school-parent relationships. Both parents and schools are strong socializing agents. Therefore, it is important that they understand each other's values, goals, and attitudes and that they are mutually supportive.

The reason for this, in turn, lies in the needs of infants and young children for consistency and continuity of care. The younger the child, the more crucial to his well being is the development of mutuality between himself and his care giver.

Previous units described the fact that in order for basic trust and positive attachments to develop, children must be cared for in a way which is predictable, consistent, and suitable to their basic temperament or individuality. There are many examples of this. The cultural orientation of a specific family might suggest that anger be handled quickly and directly. One member would tell the other exactly how he felt and then go on to another activity. It would be important for the teacher of a child from this family to know the way anger is handled. Then he or she could most appropriately respond to the child's demonstration of feelings in school. In the home backgrounds of other children, different definitions may be placed on the roles of men and women. In one family, men may be viewed primarily as providers. They may not share in household tasks which fall to the women to perform. In another family both husband and wife may both earn money and share equally in domestic tasks. To respect the life-styles of each family, teachers and child care staff must be sensitive. For example, they should not say, "Girls don't do that," when an activity has customarily been performed by girls in the family. As a final illustration, a mother may have a particular way of holding her baby when she feeds and cares for him. If the baby is also being cared for by others, then they should also try to hold the baby in the same way his mother does.

It is extremely important that those persons who are responsible for caring for children develop ways of working with each other. By providing consistent care, they can meet their shared goal of promoting the children's positive development. Since each adult human being is a unique individual himself, with personal viewpoints and practices, development of *collaboration* (teamwork) is not easy. It requires special sensitivity and commitment. The following sections describe some of the characteristics of parent-teacher contacts and ways which have been found to make them productive.

COMMUNICATION

One essential mode of collaboration between parties concerned with child care is communication. This includes sharing and exchanging important information and the joint planning of experiences and approaches. It should be mentioned that the attitudes and child rearing practices of everyone having contact with a specific child do not have to be totally identical or perfectly coordinated. Children should experience differences among people with whom they interact as well as similarities. They need to recognize that others have different ways.

Without communication, a meaningful arrangement of experiences for the children is impossible to achieve. Since communication is so important among those working with children, the processes which are involved in making it effective must be understood. Thorough understanding reduces the possibility that messages are not given or that they are distorted. There are two kinds of communication (interpersonal and structural) which are helpful when working with children and families.

Interpersonal Communciation

Interpersonal communication refers to the face-to-face exchange between children, either one-to-one or in groups. It is not difficult to recognize that there are factors which can make interpersonal communication either positive or negative. Understanding these factors can help reduce barriers.

Identification With Children. Interestingly, one factor which often creates communication problems between parents and the school staff is the fact that each party may see things primarily from the point of view of the children. This identification with the children on the part of a teacher means that frequently they cannot see things from the stance of other adults. It is difficult for them to be objective about their actions or motivations.

Persons deciding to undertake professional work with young children usually do so because they like children and want to improve their lives. Such people may, for example, recall their own childhoods. Perhaps they had an unpleasant time — unstable family, "cold" parents, or "mean" teachers. Such situations may have had such a great impact on them that they want to make sure that no other child has to suffer what they did. Others may have very positive memories of their childhoods. Thus, they want to make sure that other children receive these same opportunities and beneficial relationships.

These are perfectly respectable motivations. It is necessary to have a strong drive towards undertaking work with children. The work can be difficult and frustrating, as well as gratifying. As a result of their strong feelings about the needs of children, which may arise from their own childhood experiences, professionals sometimes have a tendency to take a negative attitude towards parents. If they feel that the child's best interest has not been served, this may be justified. Often such feelings may be more intense than the situation warrants, however.

This strong feeling of identification with the children can contribute to communication problems in several ways. While parents certainly do play a key role, it has been demonstrated that there is not always a one-to-one causal relationship between parental behavior and children's characteristics. This may be difficult for teachers and others professionally involved with the child to accept in the face of problem behavior. If a child comes to school upset, it is easiest to say, "something must be going on at home." If a child is wearing unkempt clothing, it is easy, again, to interpret this as meaning that the parents "don't even care how he looks." Single cause thinking such as this can be detrimental to communication. It leads the workers to avoid trying to assess what the situation really is. Perhaps the upset child was "picked on" by another child in the bus, or perhaps the parent of the child wearing messy clothing was sick and unable to finish the wash. When sufficient information is not available, situations involving the children and their families are not handled as effectively as they should be. Teachers who search for all of the facts by instituting a process of communication are more likely to handle them with understanding and appropriate methods.

Attitudes Towards Parents. Parents are able to pick up "blaming" attitudes on the part of the school staff and are acutely sensitive to them. The attitude towards parents which has been prevalent for some time has caused parents to be very self-conscious about their child rearing practices. If they receive the impression that teachers are critical of them, this causes another communication problem. The parents may become reluctant to offer information, to voice their concerns, to seek the advice of school personnel, and to act on their suggestions.

Attitudes Towards Experts. Parents themselves may have *ambivalent* (both positive and negative) attitudes towards those who work with their children. On one hand, they may really wish to have information and guidelines which help them deal with day-to-day living with and planning for their child. On the other hand, they may be wary and possibly resentful of those whose position seems to suggest that they are experts in child care. With the development of the mass media, the numerous books and articles on how to raise children, professional disciplines for work

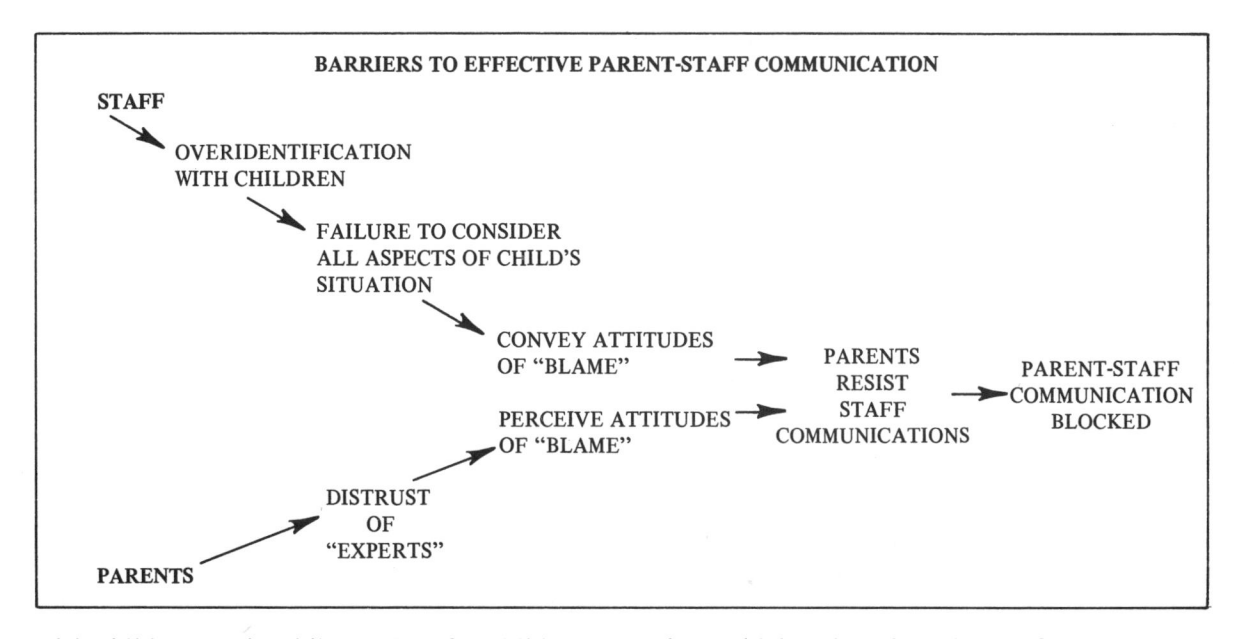

Unit 8 Establishing Parent-Teacher Contacts

```
BARRIERS TO EFFECTIVE PARENT-STAFF COMMUNICATION

STAFF
   ↘
     OVERIDENTIFICATION
     WITH CHILDREN
        ↘
          FAILURE TO CONSIDER
          ALL ASPECTS OF CHILD'S
          SITUATION
             ↘
               CONVEY ATTITUDES
               OF "BLAME"         →   PARENTS
                                      RESIST        →  PARENT-STAFF
               PERCEIVE ATTITUDES →   STAFF            COMMUNICATION
               OF "BLAME"             COMMUNICATIONS   BLOCKED
             ↗
          DISTRUST
          OF
          "EXPERTS"
        ↗
PARENTS
```

with children, and public services for children, there also came a devaluation of the role of parents. Of course these are highly positive advances, but the impact on parents also needs to be recognized. Parents feel that their opinions about their children no longer seem to hold as much weight. This has caused a distrust of so called experts by many parents. These parents develop the attitude that "book learning" and experience with other people's children do not necessarily mean that the professionals understand all children better. Whether or not the parents' feelings are valid is not the issue at hand. Rather, the presence of the feelings needs to be recognized by those who intend to develop truly positive communication with parents.

Breaking Down Communication Barriers

There are ways that these underlying dynamics of parent-staff communication can be handled in order to break down potential barriers:

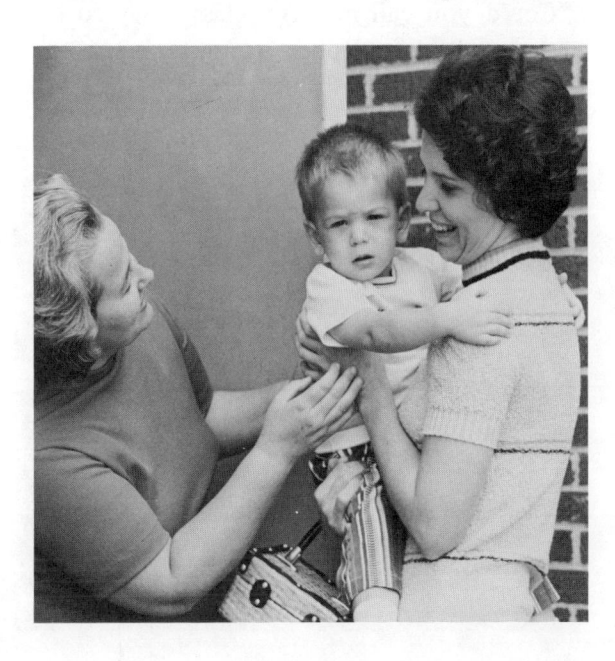

Establishing Contacts. One major means of establishing positive communication with parents is through the way brief encounters are structured. Such exchanges of information which take place in brief contacts can gradually establish a mutual respect and comfortable relationship between the parties involved. Many of these transactions can take place at the time parents bring in or call for a child. The parents may say to the person "receiving" him, "Jimmy didn't get much sleep last night," or "Jane's father just left on a two week trip." These pieces of information help the teacher know what is taking place in the child's life. The teacher may respond "We'll keep an eye on him to see if he looks tired," or "If she talks about him, we'll remind her that he'll be back in two weeks." Supportive comments convey to the parent that the teacher feels that they are in a collaborative relationship to benefit the child. When parents pick up their children, the teacher might remark, "Mary really enjoyed using the workbench today," or "Terry ate all of his lunch." These factual reports, which do not necessarily have to grow out a "crisis" situation, provide interesting information for the parents. They also show the children themselves that those people who are most responsible for their care share their concerns for them by talking with each other.

Incidental contact, then, can be used for communication around matters of mutual interest which do not necessarily signal the need for specific action or intervention. It is disquieting for a parent picking up a child if the teacher says, "We really need to do something about Robert's aggression." This makes it difficult for the parent to respond. Others may be around or neither party may have time for quiet discussion. It would be more appropriate for the teacher to say under these circumstances, "Could you call me after class today so that we can talk about Robert's progress in school?"

Choice of Language. Child care staff, in talking with parents, should use appropriate language. It should not be so simple that it appears to condescend to the parent, nor should it be overloaded with technical jargon. For example, it might be best if the teacher stated, "Johnny sometimes has trouble telling other children how he feels," rather than, "Johnny seems to have an impairment of his affective expression." "We enjoy hearing Joan discuss some of the experiences she's had at home" is more appropriate than, "It's obvious that Joan comes from a stimulating, cognitively oriented home environment." In general, language which is plain, direct, and specific is the most helpful and the least threatening to parents.

Respect for Parents' Opinions. Smooth communication with parents is encouraged by showing respect for their opinions. Parents are highly sensitive to an "I understand him better than you do" attitude on the part of a teacher. As a result, communication is shut off. Neither party receives the information needed to be helpful to the child. Respect for parents' opinions can be conveyed in various ways.

It is wise to avoid providing explanations for a child's behavior without gathering the parent's input first. A staff member may open a conference by saying, "We feel that Joe's problems are caused by something going on at home." The parent is then likely to become defensive, at best. He or she may reply, "We thought it was something here at school." The staff member may say, instead, "Joe seems to be more tense lately. Have you noticed anything different?" The parent, who may indeed have observed similar behavior, may welcome the opportunity for joint discussion and planning.

The teacher may ask the parent's ideas on handling puzzling or difficult behavior which takes place in school. Here, she might say, in a discussion of a child's quietness in the classroom, "Do you have any suggestions which might help us draw Jim out a little bit?" "What do you do when Johnny is worried?", not only creates a feeling in the parent that he is respected, but also may provide some truly valuable and useful information about the child. After all, no matter what lacks parents may have, they are still the ones who have lived with their children over the years. They have the most direct contact with them and, therefore, knowledge of what affects their behavior.

Empathizing With Parents. Empathizing with parents is not a concrete action or form of communication. Rather, it is the specific attempt to cultivate a sensitivity to the background, attitudes, goals, and living conditions of parents. It involves being able to see things from their point of view as well as one's own. Being able to do this means that the teacher is more likely to accept the parents' viewpoints, rather than impose his own on them. There is no established way to develop empathy. It emerges from experience, knowledge of people in all their complexity, and the ability to grow and be continually open to change.

Structural Communication

Structural communication refers to those activities which provide a supportive context for interpersonal communication. They contribute a setting which should make the face-to-face quality of communication productive.

Individual Parent-Teacher Meetings. Parent-teacher meetings offer an appropriate setting for exchanging information accumulated over a period of time or for discussion of problem areas. It is important that the conditions of the meeting create a relaxed atmosphere which encourages discussion. Interruptions or physical discomfort can detract from the success of the meeting. For example, sitting in child-size furniture in the classroom is not always the best way to have a serious meeting with a parent. It might be better to use a quiet library or office. Some parents, who may previously have had negative experiences with agencies which conducted business in austere offices, may relax more in a different setting. Others are comfortable in offices, and such a meeting site is not a barrier to communication.

Written Communications. Too often, teaching staff view the formally established parent conferences, as the only means of communication available. Written communications as well can both increase understanding between parents and staff and contribute towards greater effectiveness and efficiency. Time can be freed for teachers to discuss individual matters with parents if written materials are used to convey program and other factual information.

Many programs have found parent handbooks a valuable aid to communication. These may contain such information as the background and philosophy of the school, a description of the daily program, logistic information such as times, places, telephone numbers, transportation suggestions, resources available through the program, staff listings, and meeting dates. Such publications are tremendously effective in establishing a mutually understood base of information. After parents receive the written information, they utilize individual contact for special matters.

Newsletters are another helpful form of written communication. They are especially effective in conveying periodic announcements, staff biographies, and ideas for home play and activities. They help keep parents "in touch" with the program.

Telephone Calls. Telephone calls have seldom been viewed as a means of facilitating school-home communication, yet there is evidence that phone calls encourage positive parent-teacher relationships. These calls are particularly helpful to those parents who cannot often come to school themselves in that they provide a means for two-way communication. Gotkin[1] also points out that phone calls can be used to communicate positive events around the child and to show interest and concern around other family members.

Films and Videotapes. Films and videotapes are also gaining recognition as a communication tool in early childhood programs. If a school has appropriate equipment available, such media can be used not only as a means of publicly displaying the program, but also as a basis for working with individual parents.

A study of the use of videotapes in parent conferences was made at the San Fernando Valley College Preschool.[2] It was found that because of their objectivity and visual evidence, they were most valuable as a means of positively structuring parent-teacher conferences. It was pointed out that decreasing expense of technical equipment and the fact that children do not seem to be made uncomfortable by the presence of the equipment are reasons underscoring consideration of its use. Schools should be careful to secure parental permission prior to videotaping their children, however.

SUMMARY

This unit has described the importance of parent-teacher communications in carrying out an effective program for young children. Such collaboration is essential to provide children the consistency and predictability they need for healthy development. Dynamics of interaction between parents and staff which are related to communication include identification with children and attitudes towards experts. Ways of improving interpersonal, or face-to-face, communication are (1) establishing contacts, (2) use of language, (3) respecting parent's opinions, and (4) empathizing with parents. Structural methods for establishing communication are (1) parent-teacher meetings, (2) newsletters, (3) telephone calls, and (4) videotapes.

SUGGESTED ACTIVITIES

- With a classmate or colleague, role-play a parent-teacher conference. One person acts as the teacher; the other, the parent. The teacher should bring up with the parent a "problem" he or she perceives in the child. When the "conference" is over, the parent and teacher should exchange the feelings they experienced during the conference and relate them to points made in this unit.

- If possible, assist a preschool program, with which you have an association, in the design and preparation of a newsletter for parents. What materials do you think will be of greater interest and value to the parents in terms of increasing staff-parent communication?

- Examine your own attitudes towards parents. List specific ways you can increase your sensitivity to parents and their own unique backgrounds.

[1] Lassar G. Gotkin, "The Telephone Call: The Direct Line from Teacher to Family." *Young Children*, December, 1968, pp. 270-274.

[2] E. Brady, D. Deustch, K. Farr, and B. Gold "The Use or Videotapes in Parent Conferences." *Young Children*, May, 1968, pp. 276-280.

- Obtain permission from a preschool in which you are working to make a telephone call to a parent to describe an interesting activity of the child in school. Describe the parent's reactions and your feelings regarding its contribution to effective communication.

REVIEW

A. Indicate the Best choice for each of the following.

1. Parents
    a. Are usually to blame for their children's problems in school.
    b. Always feel positive towards those working with their children.
    c. Like to have others listen to their opinions regarding their children.
    d. Respect the use of highly technical language in staff descriptions of their children.

2. Which of the following statements is not true?
    a. Parents and teachers must have identical attitudes for positive development to occur in children.
    b. Schools and other institutions play a considerable role in the development of children today.
    c. Teachers need to know how feelings are handled in the child's home.
    d. Staff should make a particular effort to hold infants the way their mothers do.

B. Briefly answer each of the following.

1. Describe the relationship of adult identification with children to communication problems between parents and teachers.
2. Describe and give examples of the kinds of language that facilitate parent-staff communications.
3. List and define four structural aids to parent-staff communication. Give the contribution made by each.
4. Describe and give examples of two ways of showing respect for parents' opinions.

unit 9 parent involvement

OBJECTIVES

After studying this unit, the student should be able to

- List and describe models of parent involvement, such as modes of parental participation in policymaking, in direct programming, and in provision of program support.
- Define the term "parent cooperative."
- Describe historical sources of parent involvement in contemporary child care programs.
- Describe some dynamics of parent involvement.

For many years, the planning and carrying out of programs for children was mainly done by those offering the service — the professionals. The parents of the children had very little to say about the services they received. This practice was based on the assumption that only professionally trained people knew what children and parents wanted and needed and how to provide it.

The advent in the 1960s of the antipoverty movement and the inception of Head Start (previously described) brought about a new concept — parent involvement. It has brought a new perspective to the issues of control and delivery of services to children and families.

PARENT INVOLVEMENT DEFINED

Basically, parent involvement means that those who use the programs participate in conduct of the programs at all levels. Parents may help in planning, policymaking, and providing resources and may actually serve as staff members.

The institution of the various forms of parent involvement emerges from several sources. The social activism of many parents, particularly minority groups, which accompanied the antipoverty movement encouraged parent involvement. People began to feel that they had previously been forced to accept service models and child caring philosophies developed by others. These groups felt that legislators and professionals were not concerned with what parents felt was needed. In addition, they felt that professionals did not know what would best serve the children in terms of the particular cultural style and goals of the parents. As a result, the movement towards insisting that consumer input be made in the design and conduct of programs intended for them grew. The intent was that the programs would reflect what minority groups wanted and felt they needed to promote both individual and group advancement. Many parents resented the implication that programs were being developed for them because of inadequacies in their performance as parents or deficits in their children. This contributed to their growing determination to voice their own wishes for the programs which would serve them.

Societal changes in the status of the family as described earlier also encouraged parent involvement. As mothers, in particular, have become increasingly interested in working or participating in other activities outside of the home, the lack of substitute child care services has become increasingly apparent. Thus, parents themselves have become interested in developing the services they need, or in seeing that those already available are suitable for them.

Another source of the emerging parent involvement movement was legislative. When federal or governmental funds are supplied for human service programs, these programs must conform to preestablished guidelines. In order to receive the money, the program actually must carry out the objectives set out for it by the funding agency. The funding for major early child care programs carried the mandate that each program include a "parent involvement component." Programs utilizing these funds had to demonstrate that there would be parent involvement of various kinds, including parent representation in policymaking bodies.

The rationale for the requirement of parent involvement came from two sources. One was the growing evidence that the early years of childhood were highly significant in terms of later development. Recognition of the fact that the quality of parent-child interaction at this time had particular influence on the cognitive ability necessary for educational achievement also played a part. For developmental and educational goals to be met through the programs, it was felt to be necessary for the role of the parents in the lives of their children to be increased. One of the major tasks of the programs was to encourage this.

The acceptance of the importance of parental linkages with early childhood programs spread widely. Today there are few programs which do not contain provision for parent participation in both planning and execution.

FORMS OF PARENT INVOLVEMENT

There are several forms of parent involvement. Parent involvement can be seen as falling into three categories when the program is sponsored by a specific organization and is professionally administered. Parents take part in policymaking, the direct program, and providing program support services. Another form of parent involvement is the *parent cooperative,* a program which is initiated and administered by parents themselves.

Participation in Policymaking

In one mode of parent participation, parents have the opportunity to contribute their opinions on basic operating matters concerning philosophy and administration. They have voting power in the decision making process as well. This mode of participation is usually achieved through some form of group membership.

Board of Directors. One form of group membership involves parents on boards of directors. These boards play a crucial role in the ongoing conduct of any program. They carry legal responsibility for the program. They are responsible for basic policymaking, hiring of executive staff, financial support, community relationships, and other essential factors. In this way, the program experiences continuity. Today, whether or not it is required by legislation, the by-laws of most boards officially provide for a number of membership spaces

Section 4 Parent-Teacher Contacts

designated to be filled by parents. By-laws establish guidelines for the basic structuring and functioning of the boards. Membership on a board of directors carries with it a considerable amount of power.

Advisory Boards. Parents also serve on advisory or consultative boards. Such boards have a somewhat different form and purpose than a governing board of directors. Advisory boards usually exist separately. They are constituted in order to provide the administration additional points of view and guidance in the conduct of the program. For example, advisory boards may provide suggestions on curriculum design, development of program resources, and utilization of staff. Program administrators or directors may solicit input from the advisory board but are not required to follow it if they do not wish. Advisory board membership provides another opportunity for parental voice. It does not, however, hold the mandated role in control which is afforded by board of director membership. Parent membership on these boards is a fairly recent occurrence.

Participation in Program

Parent involvement sometimes means the direct participation of parents in conducting some aspect of the program — either through working directly with children or through providing some type of background or supportive service.

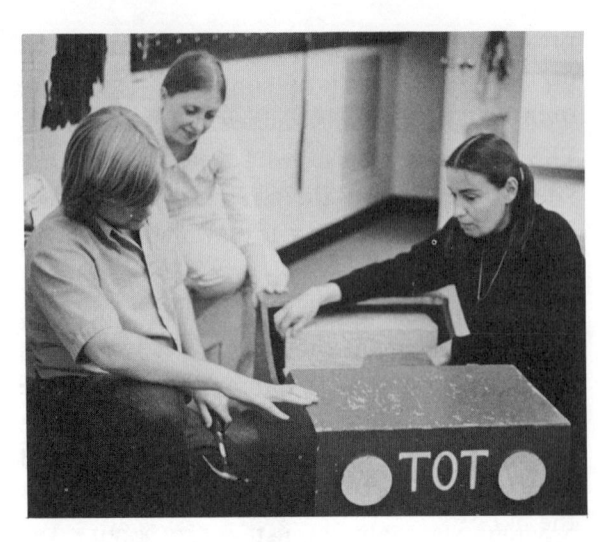

In some centers, parents may be seen involved in all classroom activities. They may do this on a rotating basis, with a parent joining the paid teaching staff each day as a volunteer. This particular form of classroom participation is often carried out when there is an actual need for additional adult supervision of children. Some centers also use this as a means to help parents understand the program better so that they can support its benefits at home.

A more frequently observed mode of direct parent involvement in classroom conduct is that which takes place when parents lead specific activities. Perhaps these activities are those in which the parents have special talents; or, the activities may be "special" to the program and can only be carried out with extra help. An example is when parents accompany the children on excursions into the community. In some programs, outings are viewed as a means of involving the parents with their children's activities and those of the community itself.

Program Support

A third mode of parent involvement consists of activities that parents perform which provide service and support to the program but do not include direct interaction with the children. Such activities may be oriented towards supplying and maintaining materials and equipment for the program. Parents may save scrap materials or donate certain kinds of supplies which are needed. In some agencies, parents supply the snacks. To help economize on equipment maintenance, parents may periodically convene to repair toys and paint the "large muscle" equipment such as the climbing boards and rocking boats. Parental efforts often are used to generally upgrade the physical environment.

Parents may also contribute some of the administrative work essential to the program. For example, they may answer the telephone, run duplicating equipment, purchase and prepare the snacks, and supervise transportation.

Fund raising is another program support form of parent involvement. In many centers, parents play an important role in organizing and conducting projects. Income from these is allocated to help continue the program. There are many ways they do this. They may hold plant sales, bake sales, rummage sales, flea markets, festivals, and small carnivals. Other forms of fund raising which parents may use include holding suppers, sponsoring entertainment programs, selling crafts made by the parents themselves or by community artisans.

In some settings, active parents have implemented funding at the wider community level. Their activities have included soliciting donations from community leaders and corporations and encouraging the passing of legislation to support child care programs. By keeping abreast of community and governmentally based funding sources and encouraging the child care center administration to take advantage of them, parents have contributed to financial resources of programs in which they are interested.

Parent Cooperatives

Parent cooperatives, in contrast to professionally organized programs in which parents may have the previously described forms of involvement, are initiated and carried out by parents themselves. While parent cooperatives may often hire teachers and other professional staff to conduct their program, administration is in the hands of the parents.

Parent cooperatives take different forms. One model is similar to professionally sponsored programs. The location of the program may be in a church or other community site. Teaching may be provided by one parent or a team of parents, but may very well be done by a professional teacher. This teacher, hired by the parents, has all of the professional knowledge and qualifications for the role.

Some smaller parent cooperative programs are conducted in homes, rather than community sites. In this model, the location may be the same home all the time or may be rotated among the homes of the cooperating parents. In the latter case, the children may be at one house on specified days and at another on others. Often the "home" parent, whose own child is usually in the program, serves as teacher for the day.

Most parent cooperatives, like any program for young children, attempt to provide opportunity for play and socialization for the participating children. As with some forms of parent involvement in community based programs, many parents in parent cooperatives also find new opportunities for stimulating their own personal growth. Previously unrecognized talents in areas such as organization, fund raising, working with people, and others frequently surface among parents who are working together to provide a sound program for their children.

DYNAMICS OF PARENT INVOLVEMENT

There is no doubt that the advent and implementation of parent involvement has made a significant contribution to improving the quality of important school-home relationships. Steps have been made towards breaking down parent-staff barriers. Parents gain in their own development as well as facilitating that of their children.

Through observation and participation in programs, parents have come to better understand their value for the children served. For example, the often-heard parental comment, "The children only play, they don't learn anything" is frequently changed after the parents watch the children play, and perhaps use the play materials themselves. These experiences help them see how learning takes place through play activities.

Through their involvement in program activities, parents may expand their current skills or become aware of brand new potentials in themselves. The parent who successfully organizes and conducts a fund-raising drive may discover administrative abilities which, when recognized by others, lead into paying work. A parent who finds he or she enjoys and does well in classroom assistance, may decide to undertake professional preparation for a teaching career. This is one of the best "by-products" of parent involvement. Nothing is a more positive influence in the life of a child than a parent who feels important and competent.

Programs in general are strengthened as a result of parent involvement. When supported by both parents and staff, they are broadened and have more strength and visibility in the community. If, for example, funding were threatened, parents themselves could organize and demonstrate against the cutbacks, indicating that they simply would not accept such action. In many instances, parental conviction and persistence in such cases has resulted in the restoration of the withdrawn resources.

However, there are some interpersonal aspects of parent involvement which must be recognized by those concerned with carrying out a truly effective parent involvement program. Token acceptance is not enough to truly achieve worthwhile goals.

To some professionals, the concept of parent involvement has posed a threat, because this has meant that their previous unilateral control of policymaking and program conduct has been challenged. These persons may have subtly tried to undermine the input of parents, so that their impact would be diminished. For example, parents might be invited to board membership, but their advice and suggestions not really taken into consideration when decisions were made. Since parents are quick to perceive whether staff really means what it says about parent involvement or if it is only being given "lip service," resentment can quickly develop if the parents feel the staff really does not plan to listen to them.

Difficult interpersonal relationships can develop among the parents themselves in all forms of parent involvement, including parent cooperatives. Some parents are more verbal and aggressive than others and may attempt to pass off their own personal viewpoints and wishes as representative of those of all the parents. Some parents may feel that one or two others are grasping and assuming leadership rather than letting it emerge naturally. It is important for staff to be sensitive to the possibility that the parent who talks the most or "gets the closest to them" may not reflect the opinions of the majority.

Disagreements over the philosophy and curriculum sometimes develop among parents. Some parents may feel, for example, that a program should directly teach academic skills, while others feel a play-oriented curriculum is more appropriate. Discipline is another area in which parents often disagree. Here, the fact that many parents do not have knowledge of child development further complicates the situation. Opinions may be strong and voiced loudly, without necessarily having a factual base.

As staff develops skills in working with parents, they may better see the collaborative aspect of their role. They may come to feel more comfortable in working with parents and dealing with some of the interpersonal dynamics which inevitably develop. Recognition of the contribution parent involvement makes to the development of both children and parents can help professionals not just to accept parent involvement but to actually encourage it as an essential part of the program.

As they orient their conception of their profession to encompass the totality of human development, they should become increasingly more comfortable with parent involvement.

SUMMARY

A trend in child development programming in recent years has been towards increasing parent involvement. This is the direct participation of program consumers in the planning and conduct of activities which previously were the sole province of the professional staff Parent involvement takes three forms: participation in policymaking participation in program, and program support.

Parent involvement has many positive by-products. Parents come to understand their children's program better; this has positive effects on the children. At the same time, the parents may discover new potential and ability in themselves.

Interpersonal difficulties can develop around parent involvement as a result of resistant staff and of self-appointed spokesmen among the parents who may lack knowledge of child development.

With sensitivity, perception, and conviction as to the benefits of parent involvement on the part of both staff and parents, this key concept in contemporary child care should continue to show positive effects and gain increasing acceptance.

SUGGESTED ACTIVITIES

- Visit several child development centers. Talk with staff about their ways of implementing parent involvement and their feelings about its advantages and disadvantages. What differences exist among the centers in modes of parent involvement and staff attitudes towards it?

- Obtain permission to attend a board meeting of a child development center in which there is parent representation. Observe the parents in particular. How much do they contribute to discussion? How is their input accepted by others? Does one parent do most of the talking, or

Section 4 Parent-Teacher Contacts

do all join in? Describe the "dynamics" among staff and parents as you observe them at this center.

- Attend a fund-raising event promoted by parents. Observe the parents to determine what specific contributions various ones have made to the event and how they organized it.

- Arrange an interview with a parent who is active in parent involvement at an early childhood center. How does the parent feel this activity has affected the development of his/her child, the rest of the family, and his/her own personal development and self-esteem? How does the parent perceive the center's attitude towards parent involvement?

- Visit a parent cooperative. What form does the program take? Is the teaching done by the parents or a professional? How are decisions made regarding the overall administration of the program? Compare the program with other preschool programs you have observed.

REVIEW

A. Define each of the following.
    1. Parent involvement
    2. Advisory board
    3. Parent cooperative

B. Indicate the best choice for each of the following.
    1. A major reason for the inclusion of parent involvement components in contemporary child care programs is that
        a. Teachers wanted parents to help them with their work.
        b. Parents were bored and wanted something to do.
        c. Children would not stay in class unless their parents were there.
        d. Funding agencies require it.
    2. An occurrence which is the most likely to cause difficulty in parent involvement programs is
        a. Children "act up" when their parents are around.
        b. Some professional staff may subtly undermine parent involvement activities.
        c. Most parents really do not want to be involved.
        d. Funding sources no longer require parent involvement.
    3. Which of the following is not a positive by-product of successful parent involvement programs?
        a. Parents understand the program better.
        b. Parents increase their own self-concept.
        c. Parents recognize that there is no role for professional staff.
        d. Parents become politically active on behalf of human service programs.

4. Which of the following parent involvement activities does not fall in the category, "program participation activities?"

   a. Serving as a board member.
   b. Conducting a carpentry lesson.
   c. Preparing and serving snacks.
   d. Supervising the painting area.

5. The parent involvement activity which falls in the category of "program support" is

   a. Serving as a board member.
   b. Maintaining equipment.
   c. Donating snacks.
   d. Duplicating materials used in the administration of the program.

6. Three parents are attending a board meeting of an early childhood center. One parent consistently interjects opinions and ideas; the others remain silent. Staff should assume that

   a. The one parent is the spokesperson for the entire parent group.
   b. The other parents are tired tonight.
   c. The one parent understands the program best.
   d. The one parent may not represent everyone's opinion.

7. A major difference between parent cooperatives and other preschool programs is

   a. There are no interpersonal difficulties among parents in parent cooperatives.
   b. There are no benefits to parents who participate in parent cooperatives.
   c. Administration is by the parents themselves in parent cooperatives.
   d. Curriculum is informally executed in parent cooperatives.

unit 10 parent education

OBJECTIVES

After studying this unit, the student should be able to

- Describe some of the historical forces which have contributed to a need for parent education.
- List and describe various current models of parent education programs.
- Discuss considerations which govern the establishment and conduct of parent education programs.
- List the steps to be taken in setting up a parent education program.

The term *parent education* refers to a variety of means used to guide parents so that they can raise their children as effectively as possible. Parent education is different from therapy. Parent education is geared towards providing information about children which can then be used by parents in better understanding and managing them. Therapy is oriented towards the exploration of deep-level feelings.

Frequently, parents turn to early childhood education and day care centers for assistance in dealing with their children. Parent education programs are also developed and offered by social agencies and other community institutions. The programs may be open just to parents of children served by the agency or school, or they may be open to the wider community.

HISTORY OF PARENT EDUCATION

To best understand the concerns of modern parents for whom parent education programs are intended, it is important to examine first the history of parenting practices in this country. The development of American society is closely tied in with the ways in which parents have raised their young and the help they have needed and sought in doing so.

In the earliest days of life in America, parent education was simple indeed. Biblical writings about raising children, such as "Spare the rod...," and their own memories of childhood were major sources of parental guidance. Most important was the fact that in frontier days, relatives usually lived with a family. A puzzled mother had her own mother or a favorite aunt to "turn to" when she needed child rearing advice. Thus, in the absence of the mass media which today convey the findings and opinions of child rearing scholars, parents could turn to their own extended families. These relatives were living right under the same roof and were willing to pass on their own child rearing traditions. These large families were close as they all joined together in the difficult fight to forge a living from the land.

After the Industrial Revolution, when machines and city life began drawing people away from farm life, sources of guidance for parents dried up for a while. Taking factory jobs in growing cities, young people no longer had the support and tradition of the relatives they left behind to rely on. Young mothers, now left alone in the house while their husbands went off to "blue collar" or office jobs, needed something else to answer their questions about raising children.

At the same time families were beginning to live in these new ways, the science of psychology was developing. New ways of looking at human development and behavior gradually became known. One of these was John Watson's *Behaviorism,* which contended that children could be carefully trained to behave as adults wanted them to. Another was the well-known psychoanalytic theory of Sigmund Freud, which stressed the importance of early experiences in the family for later adult personality. As parents became exposed to these new approaches from outside, they began to question, rather than accept, their own ways. They became eager consumers of the growing body of published work on child development and child guidance. Thus, parent education became a recognized activity among the growing body of services society provided for children.

Even before the parent education movement became widespread, there were some efforts to provide materials on child raising. The Child Study Association of America, which has offices in New York, was founded in 1888 by a group of mothers who wanted to learn how they could do a better job as parents. This association is still active and is highly respected for its contribution to the field of parent education. In the early 1900s, the United States government began publication of widely circulated pamphlets offering parental guidance. *Infant Care,* periodically updated, is an example of one of these. Later on, in the 1950s, books such as the famous *Baby and Child Care* by Dr. Benjamin Spock appeared — adding to the variety of widely available resources for parents.

Early childhood development began to come into its own during the 1960s, under the influence of the War on Poverty. The Head Start program was designed to provide learning experiences to children before school entrance. The activity of some women to achieve greater participation in the world outside the home pressed for recognizing the needs of mothers for help in child raising. In addition to the interest being shown in the role of parental practices and early experiences in child rearing, there is also a mounting interest in parent education.

CURRENT FORMS OF PARENT EDUCATION

Many parents have expressed a need for help with the job of raising their children. Several different ways of providing parents with information have been developed.

Individual Parent-Teacher Conferences

Many schools schedule individual conferences with parents for the purpose of discussing matters of mutual concern and a child's progress in the program. The parent may initiate these, but often the school does, offering each parent the opportunity to come to the school. Such contacts are important. They not only help the parent feel welcome and valued, but also frequently provide an opportunity for exchanges which might be considered parent education. Many parents regard their children's teacher — particularly a preschool teacher — as the person to turn to when they have questions about their children's development. Parents may say: "Should Janie still be sucking her thumb?", "Why do children play with water?", "Johnny seems to have trouble sharing." The exchange which takes place between the parent and the teacher provides helpful guidelines for parents.

Parent Rooms or Parent Corners

Recognizing both the need for and interest in parent education, many schools set up special areas on the premises in which parents can stop while their children are in school. Such areas may be stocked with a coffee pot, comfortable chairs, and shelves

Section 4 Parent-Teacher Contacts

with books and pamphlets on matters of interest to parents of young children. These provide parents the chance to get to know each other on a casual basis, as well as to have the opportunity to examine the written material. Selection of materials in the center should be based on the staff's awareness of the needs and interests of their particular group of parents. Discussing the kinds of questions parents ask in individual conferences and other informal interchanges between parents and the school staff can take place here.

Mass Media

Books, pamphlets, television, films, magazine articles, and other large scale forms of communication are vehicles of parent education. These sources are among those to which parents may turn whether or not they are made available by their child's school. For many parents, they take the place of relatives and teachers. The quality of mass media for parents varies. Some materials are developed by experienced professionals and are based on a broad knowledge of working with people. The Child Study Association of America is one of these.

Many parents get the bulk of their guidance from popular magazine articles and books. Many of these are valid and appropriate. Others may be based on a new way of thinking or a new type of research study which has not been fully tested. Such material can be confusing to parents. Lacking formal study in child development and led only by their own uncertainties, they may either misapply or too rigidly interpret what they read. One of the greatest contributions a trained teacher or parent education leader can make to parents is to help them select and suitably use good quality resources.

Parent Group Education

A general form which some parent education programs take is a series of meetings. A trained leader is in charge. Group discussions on topics on which the parents express mutual concern are encouraged. This "model" of parent education was first developed by S.W. Slavson, who is well known for his work with groups. It is still in wide use today. The focus of the discussions is on children, the giving of information which is helpful in living with and understanding them, and the sharing of experiences in parenting among the participants. It is found in such meetings that the parents themselves, simply by exchanging their own ideas of how they handled situations or of what problems they have found in working with their children, can be highly supportive of and helpful to each other.

This type of program is highly flexible and is still widely used. In recent years, in keeping with the renewed interest in parent education, some variations have been developed.

One of these is what might be called the *sequential lecture* model, in which a different person comes to the group each time to speak on some aspect of child development. Another form of parent group meetings is that in which the leader prepares a list of topics for consideration at each meeting. Perhaps he or she delivers a short lecture on the topic, with the discussion following the presentation.

Today there are some parent education programs which have been developed to express one particular philosophy or approach. One example of this is the Parent Effectiveness Training Program developed by Dr. Thomas Gordon.[1] Leaders wishing to conduct the program with a group are themselves instructed in the method at a special institute or training program prior to running a program on their own. This is different from the "parent group education" model. The latter is geared towards developing a broad based understanding of children, while the former is concerned with the training of the parent in specific skills in one area of child rearing. In the Parent Effectiveness program, the key skill is that of communication. Parents are taught how to actively listen to children and respond to them and other communication techniques which Dr. Gordon feels contribute to positive parent-child relationships.

Several approaches to parent education are designed to increase parents' effectiveness as teachers of their children, through application of principles of behavioral psychology. One program of this kind is *Teaching Parents Teaching* developed by David Champagne and Richard Goldman.[2] This is primarily geared towards teachers themselves, to help them become better teachers of parents so that the parents in turn can become more effective teachers of their own children. Its underlying premise is that the mutual concern of parents and teachers for children's learning can involve parents in supporting their school learning. By using effective teaching methods to work with their children in the home, parents increase the continuity between the children's home and school experiences.

Teaching Parents Teaching provides teachers with specific strategies for helping parents learn ways of helping their children in educational activities. Stress is made on ways of approaching parents and explaining the program to them which will encourage their wish to participate rather than cause resistance. The major tool for the parents is the use of positive reinforcement. This involves their making statements of praise in response to their children's positive attempts to learn. These *reinforcers,* or verbal rewards, increase the chance that the children will learn the behavior which was reinforced and that they will repeat it in the future.

Parents Are Teachers by Wesley Becker[3] is similar to *Teaching Parents Teaching* in that it, too, is oriented towards helping parents to be better teachers of their children through use of reinforcement techniques. However, this approach is intended to improve parents' skills in general home management of children, as well as to work with them for specifically educational purposes.

Another trend in parent education is the use of what is called an *experiential* model. This was pioneered by Dr. Tobias Brocher of Germany and is now in use in this country. It is based on the concept of experiential learning, which means that people learn effectively by active doing rather than simply talking, listening to lectures, or receiving highly structured material. Rather than just sit quietly, parents are offered the opportunity to play with materials of the same kind that

[1]Thomas Gordon. *Parent Effectiveness Training.* New York: Peter Wyden, 1970.

[2]D.W. Champagne and R.M. Goldman. *Teaching Parents Teaching.* New York: Appleton Century Crofts, 1972.

[3]Wesley C. Becker. *Parents Are Teachers.* Champaign, Ill: Research Press, 1971.

their young children receive in their classrooms. In discussion with their children following the play, parents relate the memories of their own childhood which have been recalled by the materials. Trained leadership is essential to use of this type of program.

There is a related use of the experiential model which many schools find helpful in working with parents. The parents are invited to school on an evening soon after the program begins. Rather than ask them to listen to a lecture, the school staff has them meet in the children's classroom. The room is set up with play materials and equipment arranged just as if the children were to begin the day. The parents are then invited to try the materials. After playing with them, they meet with the teachers to discuss their feelings about the experience. Many directors have found this type of meeting most helpful in terms of answering parent's questions and concerns about the school program. Some parents have questions about a school program. They may wonder, as has been stated in earlier units, why the children are "allowed" to play so much. After a chance to play themselves and to discuss their questions with the staff, they are better able to see how play helps a child learn and develop emotionally.

SELECTION AND DEVELOPMENT OF A PARENT EDUCATION PROGRAM

There are a number of points that a school staff should consider in making its choice about the kind of parent education program it wishes to conduct. Various approaches have both merits and weaknesses which should be carefully evaluated. Careful choice helps ensure that whatever program is developed is both enjoyable and effective. If parents do not learn or benefit from a program, there is little justification for holding it in the first place.

Specific needs and characteristics of parents should be considered in program planning. Many parents are quite anxious in child rearing efforts, wondering self-consciously whether or not they are doing the right thing. Other parents are not thoughtful enough about what they are doing. Wherever parents are in terms of concern about child rearing practices, however, parent education program leaders have found that many of them are hoping to find a quick or ready answer. New approaches are often seized upon by teachers, professionals, and others as well as by parents in the hope of finding this magic key.

Program planners must be careful to see that their program is not too narrow or one-sided in its coverage. Children's behavior and parents' influences on it are affected by a variety of complex factors in interaction with each other. These must all be considered in order to help parents evaluate a difficult situation. When parents find that too narrow approaches simply do not work, they often become disillusioned. Group leaders need to be careful to indicate just what application their program will have to the parents' concerns.

Like children, parents also have their own learning styles, ways in which they best take in information. Some parents enjoy listening to lectures and reading books about children. Others, however, have a more "do it" orientation to life. Such parents, in contrast to the first group, might respond better to an experientially based approach to parent education.

The fact that parents may tend to view parent educators as experts places a special responsibility on the educators. They must be careful to avoid giving answers based on insufficient knowledge of the factors involved in the parents' situation which could then be misconstrued or misused. Programs which over a period of time allow for the exploration, with others, of the many possible facets of perplexing problems can prevent this to an extent. Parent education programs which give parents greater resources with which to evaluate their own individual concerns, as well as giving them basic information, help them make the soundest use of what they learn.

A pitfall of some parent education programs is that they are too theoretical, too far removed from touching on the parents' daily experiences of living with their children. Programs which tell parents that their children need more love, need discipline and limits, need stimulation in the home must do more if these goals are to be achieved. Inclusion of practical guidelines of ways to "translate" theory into direct line practice within the home, are essential. How to help Johnny get to bed, as well as why he may not want to go and what playthings to select and how to arrange them, as well as the importance of play, are important. Leaders can encourage parents to exchange their ideas on how to handle situations in a practical way.

Programs must take into consideration the cultural differences in child rearing practices, such as those described in an earlier unit. Many attitudes towards children and ways of dealing with life differ among various groups. One group may value fairly strict discipline and limit-setting. Another may place great emphasis on a child's being able to express feelings freely. These attitudes must be respected by anyone attempting to develop a parent education program. It should be pointed out that this does not mean that the program cannot encourage growth or change in the participants. It should start where they are in such a way that they can relate the program to their own style of living and child raising, however.

The economic circumstances of the parent group should also be taken into consideration in designing a program. Chronic, severe economic deprivation and social ills in many cases puts the solution to child rearing problems outside the educative function. A mother who has no washing machine or hot water or car to get to the nearest laundromat, may not take the same developmental attitude to toilet training as does the mother with the latest washer-dryer combination at her fingertips. For such parents, it almost seems as if programs designed to help them build their own strength and skills so as to be able to alter their unfortunate circumstances would be the first "educative" priority.

Isolation is the experience of many parents today, as a result of the present structuring of today's child rearing practices. Many mothers spend the day alone in their houses with their small children. This situation in the long run cannot contribute to positive attitudes. Parent education programs can provide the means to help lonely and isolated mothers make new friends. This is in itself an achievement likely to have positive results in terms of healthy relationships between mothers and their children.

Many parent educators have found that parents are best able to respond to their offerings when the parents have the opportunity to know them over a period of time and when they can have direct contact with them. This does not meant that the relationship must be deeply personal, but simply that the parent can see the leader as a person as well as a professional. This helps to build parental trust and confidence in the leader's offerings.

Section 4 Parent-Teacher Contacts

A fault in the sequential lecture model of parent education, or in any lecture program for parents, is that the structure does not permit extended, direct contact to take place. If an agency or school were to develop a program based on different guest speakers, it would be important that one key person be present at each session. This person could help provide continuity as well as be a consistent figure with whom the participants could relate over the course of the sessions.

Finally, no matter what "model" philosophy of parent education is being employed, its stance should not be one of blaming or criticizing the parent participants. Nothing builds resistance in parents faster than leaders and material which point fingers at them as the only source of their troubles with their children. Programs which convey respect and support to parents, recognizing that they are the ones who live with the children on a twenty-four-hour basis, have the greatest chance of acceptance and of actually making an impact. The most sucessful parent educators are those who, with humility, feel that they do not have all the answers. Rather than showing one way, they help parents in finding their own.

PRACTICAL GUIDELINES IN ESTABLISHING PARENT EDUCATION PROGRAMS

The following practical guidelines may help a parent education program run smoothly.

- Selection of Staff: A school wishing to begin a parent education program first of all decides what staff it will need to run the program and what each person's role will be. For a parent group education program, a leader well-schooled in child development who also has warmth towards parents should be selected. This may be the school's director, social worker, head teacher, or other qualified person. For a lecture or series of lectures, it is often helpful to have a person take charge of making the arrangements, including contacting and introducing the speakers.

- Setting of Program Objectives: As with any course of instruction, the sponsoring group will want to define what its goals are with parents. This will naturally determine the nature and organization of the content of the program.

- Location of Resources: The persons involved in conducting the program must decide what resources they will use in the program (speakers, books, handouts) and arrange to get them. Serving refreshments has been found to help break the ice in many parent groups.

- Selection of Physical Space: There must be a place to conduct the program. Many group leaders find that a comfortable room, with a table for materials and chairs which can be drawn up to make an informal circle, is a good setting to create an atmosphere suited for a small group program.

- Publicity: If a program is intended for parents outside of one's own school, a wide program of publicity to attract participants is usually necessary. Since it takes quite a bit of effort to establish a publicity program, many schools confine the scope of their parent education efforts to the parents of the children who attend the school. They build the content and focus around their knowledge of the needs and interests of this particular group. Announcements can be sent home with the children and to other schools. Notices can be posted in supermarkets and other places where parents are likely to gather. Church bulletins, newspapers, and radio announcements are among other possible ways a sponsoring group can inform the public about its program.

Some agencies charge a modest fee for a program. This is intended both to help pay expenses and to make the participant feel committed to the program by having a financial investment in it. They also may offer scholarship help to families who need it.

ROLE OF THE ASSISTANT TEACHER IN PARENT EDUCATION

Whether or not assistant teachers or aides actually conduct or develop a series of parent group meetings, it is still helpful for them to have some awareness of the structure of various kinds of parent education programs. It is possible that as they progress in professional development, they will move in the direction of greater activity in parent education.

Assistants and aides almost always have contacts with the parents of the children in their groups. As a result, they often are asked questions. Their awareness of the relationship of these inquiries to broader aspects of parent education and to the development of parent education programs in their own school is important. Their understanding of some of the basic needs and concerns of parents for guidance with their children and of some of the resources available can help them handle inquiries in an appropriate way.

SUMMARY

In keeping with the increased recognition of the importance of positive parent-school relationships and of the needs of parents for guidance and support in child rearing, parent education programs are part of the offerings of many schools and agencies. It is important for the aide or assistant to understand some of the difficulties faced by modern parents.

Parent education may take many forms and utilize many different types of resources. Individual parent-teacher conferences, parent group meetings, and mass media are among current modes of parent education.

Many factors must be taken into consideration in developing a parent education program. Among these are parental anxiety levels, learning styles, experiences of isolation, and subcultural differences in child rearing practices.

Some parents need practical guidelines as well as theoretical material. Above all, programs must avoid implying blame or criticism of parents.

For more formalized parent education programs to be set up, there are basic guidelines that can be followed: selecting staff, setting program objectives, locating resources, developing a physical space for the program, and instituting publicity.

The understanding of the nature of parent education programs and their relationship to the needs and concerns of parents adds an important dimension to the work of assistant teachers.

SUGGESTED ACTIVITIES

- If your school does not have a formal parent education program of its own, locate another school or social agency which does. Request an appointment with a staff member to share experiences in developing and conducting parent education programs.

- Reflect on questions asked you by parents of children you have contact with, if you are already in a working situation. What is the nature of the concerns they are expressing? What type of parent education program do you think would be appropriate for them?

- Obtain a current well-known book for parents on child rearing. Evaluate it critically in terms of how well you feel it is suited to really help parents in their daily concerns.

- Assume you are a director of a preschool. The mothers have asked you for help in guiding their children at home. They have indicated that they would be willing to attend a series of meetings. Prepare a sample agenda for a series of six meetings. Provide a rationale for your choice.

- Carry out a role-played parent education group meeting. One person should be the leader, and the rest, parents. The leader should establish a general topic for discussion such as "discipline," and after speaking briefly on it, open the floor to comments and questions by the parents. Following the experience, discuss what took place in the group. What strategies did the leader use which facilitated discussion? What "group dynamics" took place among the parents? Who dealt with these, and how?

- Role play a parent teaching a child. Provide a task for the parent to teach. Whenever the child makes a positive response, the parent should praise the child. Discuss the feelings of the parent and child in this teaching situation. What is your opinion of the use of positive reinforcement in teaching? What applications does it have to various areas of child care practice?

REVIEW

A. Define each of the following.
1. Parent education
2. Parent group education
3. Experiential teaching
4. Parent effectiveness training program
5. Child Study Association of America
6. Sequential lecture model

B. Indicate the best choice for each of the following.
1. Parents often tend to view group leaders or lecturers as
   a. Uninterested.
   b. Experts.
   c. Poorly prepared.
   d. Dull.

2. A highly effective way to help parents understand the program of a school is to

   a. Go to the home and describe the program.
   b. Send each parent a brochure.
   c. Have the parents use the same materials the children do.
   d. Not try to inform parents, since they really cannot understand.

3. A danger which all parent educators must be especially careful to avoid is

   a. Being warm to the parents.
   b. Providing specific answers without gathering sufficient information.
   c. Helping parents get to know each other.
   d. Having group meetings last too long.

4. For a group of parents from poverty level incomes, the first priority in educative efforts would probably be

   a. To help them develop their own personal strengths and skills as adults.
   b. Expose them to a series of lectures on child development.
   c. Refer them to some good books.
   d. Tell them they are at fault for their troubles.

5. A healthy by-product of parent group programs is

   a. Increased income for the sponsoring agency.
   b. Reduction in isolation for many parents by helping them get acquainted with each other.
   c. Emphasis on theoretical approaches can be given.
   d. Leader can have a forum for his views.

6. All of the following can contribute to a positive parent education program except

   a. An attitude of understanding the parents' situation.
   b. Respect for cultural differences in child rearing practices.
   c. Providing practical tips as well as theoretical material.
   d. Showing parents there is only one way to do things.

7. The viewpoint on child development which underlies a sound parent education program is

   a. That parents are the sole cause of their children's behavior.
   b. That parents have nothing to do with how their children turn out.
   c. That the factors which influence the developing child are complex.
   d. That parents can succeed if they have good "book knowledge" of child development.

Section 4 Parent-Teacher

      8. The major teaching tool in those models of parent education programs which are based on behavioral psychology is

         a. Negative reinforcement.
         b. Punishment.
         c. Positive reinforcement.
         d. Food.

C. Place the following steps in organizing a parent education program in chronological order.

      a. Publicity
      b. Location of resources
      c. Setting of program objectives
      d. Staff selection
      e. Selection of physical space

unit 11   working with parents and children in the home

OBJECTIVES

After studying this unit, the student should be able to

- Describe types of programs in which child development staff work in the home setting.
- Discuss the special values of working within the home to promote sound child development and positive parent-child relationships.
- Discuss personal qualities which home visitors need to posses to be effective.
- Describe types of activities performed by home visitors.

A child care assistant may ask, "Why study ways of working in the home? I work in a classroom." There are several answers to this question.

First of all, more and more developing child care programs are based on the concept of working with children and families in the home setting. The assistant may participate in carrying out such a program. Just as likely, the assistant may be working with children who at one time have been served through a home-based program. Knowledge of ways of working with parents and children in the home will extend the skills of assistants. It will also help them to better understand the background and experiences of the children with whom they are working in the classroom.

More and more preschools and day care centers are recognizing the values of home visits to help bridge the gap between home and school. When the school staff are familiar with the child's home environment, they can better guide his classroom activity. Assistants may be asked to make home visits as part of their teaching duties.

THE NATURE OF HOME CONTACTS

The specific nature of work with families in the home depends, naturally, on the goals which are to be achieved by the program initiating the visits. Many recent child development programs have been designed to provide experiences and special support to famliles with very young children. Programs of early intervention are aimed at families which through poverty and other adverse circumstances, might have difficulty in providing the type of environment which fosters development, particularly in the cognitive (learning) area. Work in the home is one way such programs are carried out. Infant stimulation programs are an example. Here the worker visits the home and attempts to demonstrate to the mother, or prime caretaker, ways of providing the infant with a developmentally sound environment. This includes giving both personal attention and sensory experience. The home visitor might, for example, work with the mother on talking to her baby to help him develop socially and emotionally. She might also bring a new plaything for the baby and interest the mother in using it with him.

Many agencies which provide service to handicapped children, in keeping with the trend towards starting intervention at the youngest possible age, are increasingly working within the home. Here, workers may visit the family to demonstrate remediative (corrective) exercises or activities which can be done with the child by the parents. They may also gather observational information which is helpful in better understanding the child's handicap and planning for his future. Such visits also provide personal support for parents who are experiencing stress as they realize that they have a child with special needs.

Some programs such as Head Start, designed for preschool children, may include a plan for recruitment into it of children from the community. Many families whose children might benefit from such a program may either not know about it or may resist considering it. Frequently this resistance is due to lack of sufficient information or understanding of the program. Teachers or social workers representing the program may systematically visit homes in which there are known to be young children and try to interest the families in the school program.

Others in early childhood education programs may wish to select children on the basis of a study of the child's suitability for their particular program. Here again a home visit may be made to gather the kind of information the program feels will be helpful to it in making a decision. Still others use home visits as a means of trying to gain insight into as many aspects of the children in their program as possible, so that they can most effectively work with them.

Sometime during the period of a child's enrollment in a program, his family may experience a crisis. Or, a child may stop attending. Here a home visit might be made to see if the school staff can be of assistance, either in helping the child deal with the crisis or in getting the child to return to school.

Formerly much therapeutic work, or treatment, of young children with emotional problems took place in mental health agency or child guidance center offices. Now it is becoming increasingly recognized by such treatment centers that work within the home setting can be very beneficial. A more accurate picture of the child's troubled behavior can be obtained through observing him in the place where he actually spends most of his time. Ways of handling the upset child can be demonstrated rather than described to puzzled parents when the contact takes place in the child's home. Thus, home visits, frequently on a scheduled basis, are now an accepted mode of treatment in mental health agencies.

SPECIAL VALUE OF WORK IN THE HOME

Work in the home carries with it some particular advantages in improving the functioning of children and families. The lives of very young children are centered around the home and the relationships within it. The logical place to work with them, therefore, is within their own homes. In addition, when a worker comes to an infant or toddler's home, it saves the complicated effort necessary for the mother to transport him to an office in the community. This increases the probability that the program and the family can develop and maintain regular contacts. When parents are "seen" by teachers or workers in offices, they are automatically cast into a subservient role. Someone else is in control of the situation; the parent is the guest to be put at ease. This may make many parents feel self-conscious and awkward and place a restraint on communication. Parents may find it difficult to openly discuss difficult or uncomfortable feelings and situations in this setting.

Parents with modest finances, or from cultural backgrounds in which exposure to public places is minimal, may feel overwhelmed by a lushly decorated office complete with waiting room and receptionist. Some may also have a distrust of the "professional."

When a worker visits the home, however, the roles are reversed. Here the parents are "at home" in surroundings completely familiar to them. They are the ones who greet workers and help make them feel comfortable. Even workers themselves may be able to respond more warmly and humanly to their clients in a home, rather than a more formal or institutional setting. There is less likely to be the stiffly posed group, with the barrier of an office desk posing an invisible wall to openness and both psychological and physical comfort.

Too often people who work with children tend to think of the children's parents in terms of weaknesses. If the children have problems, the workers may want to blame someone for causing them. Parents are usually the targets of these feelings. Workers may state: "Jim has such a poor home situation" or "With that mother, no wonder Sara can't fit into the group." Since the major motivation of people entering the child care field is, naturally, to work directly with children, this attitude, which was discussed earlier, is understandable. It is easy to see only the needs of the children and to want to pinpoint a cause for their problems. The parents of particular children may indeed have a strong responsibility for their personality characteristics and behavior. Yet, the tendency for some child care staff to see families as "bad" or the sole cause of the children's problems is not constructive. It is difficult for those holding such an attitude to truly help both children and families.

When workers visit the child's home, however, they can see the strengths as well as the weaknesses of the family. A mother who comes across in the office as a "bland" personality may come to life in the eyes of workers when they can see her artwork on display in her living room or when they are served a slice of her freshly baked bread. They may observe, also, how well she and her husband, both of whom are working, have set up a plan for maintaining a well run household.

Workers can appreciate the problems of a mother with a *hyperactive* (overactive) child when they actually observe her trying to manage him in a tiny home where there are several other small children. In the home, ways in which parents effectively deal with crises or lack of resources can also be seen... a poverty level mother has ingeniously constructed toys out of scrap materials...a father is warm and caring to several small children while his wife is seriously ill.

The child's home, naturally, is the base from which he operates. He moves out from it to school and the wider world. Thus, it is a strong influence on his behavior as observed and dealt with by outside people. Visiting the child's home, the worker may have the opportunity to "see" a side to the child which may never be directly observed in the classroom, but which may well influence the child's behavior there.

A child's parent may tell his teacher: "Johnny fights with his sister at home," or "I can tell him to do something, and he won't listen." At Johnny's home, the worker can see just how and under what circumstances such behavior takes place. Such information can be helpful to all involved in working with the child and helping him progress.

Contact in the home helps the family and the worker to communicate effectively with each other, so that information to be conveyed is really "heard" and understood by the other party. For example, the worker can demonstrate a point she wants to make regarding the management of the child, without actually drawing attention to the fact that she is doing this. In an office conference, a teacher may say to parents, "Play with him more," or "Accept his feelings when setting limits." By the time the parents arrive home, they may have forgotten these suggestions or have little idea as to how to carry them out within the confines of their particular situation. As the worker plays with the child at home, parents can see how to involve him in play. By watching and listening to the home visitor, an approach may be adopted by parents without lengthy explanations which could be perceived as threatening or too complicated by the parents.

In addition, work within the home permits all parties to be more physically active. This too can help to break down barriers to communication. Some parents are uncomfortable simply talking or listening. In a setting where workers and parents can participate in a task together, the physical movement involved often serves to relieve feelings of awkwardness.

QUALITIES OF THE HOME VISITOR

For the many advantages of home visiting to be realized, it is necessary that the worker possess special sensitivities. People who are well-educated in the needs of children may find it difficult to accept people who may do things they think are not helpful to the children. Often workers must see parents treat their children in ways they feel they would like to change quickly. Workers, in their wish to alter parental behavior, may react hastily, behaving in a judgmental and disapproving way. This only serves to close the parents to what the workers are saying. It is necessary to accept parents where they are when undertaking work with them. Press for change should take place at a rate that will not alienate or threaten the parents.

Differences between the parents and the worker in income level and cultural background are related to the factor of acceptance. Poverty level families may be self-conscious about the furnishings of their home. The worker must avoid conveying criticism either directly or subtly. Other families, as a culturally based characteristic, may find it difficult to accept help. (Usually the fact of making a home visit implies that the family is in need of some kind of assistance which the worker will help to provide.) Such families out of their tradition feel that to need help is to lose face. They feel that this makes a strong definition of their inadequacy, even though it is not truly the case. Still other families may not want to talk with workers. This again may be due to their own family tradition of "keeping our troubles to ourselves" rather than a specific wish to be uncooperative or unfriendly.

Part of the initial acceptance of the family as they are implies that workers will try to be alert to differences in backgrounds between the two. Workers must avoid interpreting the family's behavior in terms of their own culturally-based values.

When workers — professionals and assistants — share the same class or cultural background as the child and family, they may find that they are more readily accepted. This is not to say, however, that workers must always be of the same background as the families with whom they are working. Many workers have been able to extablish strong and effective working relationships with families of different backgrounds. Qualities of patience, sensitivity, and warmth and a solid understanding of child development, coupled with the recognition that change is slow, make this possible.

Accepting parents where they are and respecting cultural factors does not mean that workers close their eyes to parental behavior which is harmful to the child. There are some child rearing practices which are destructive to the child no matter what the cultural background of the family is. The worker must recognize these. For example, a child whose attempts to communicate are always misunderstood or are met with an abrupt response is negatively influenced, even if the style of the family is to act rather than to talk or listen. Some cultural groups rely more on physical punishment to guide and correct their children than do others. No matter what the family's prevalent attitudes and practices are regarding physical punishment, however, the child who is subjected to ongoing and severe physical punishment is harmed. In such cases, workers are faced with a difficult dilemma in which they must strike a very delicate balance between acceptance and insistence on constructive change.

The tendency for people committed to working in the field of child development and child care to identify primarily with the needs of children is, as has been mentioned, common. The mature worker should recognize that the parents have needs, too — for interesting activity, for enjoyment of life's pleasures, for the feeling that they, too, are worthy and growing people. Unfortunately, many grown people have not had the educational, social, and financial opportunities which contribute towards "the good life." Their lives may be full of frustration, struggles for day-to-day survival, futility, anger, and disruption. To effectively serve such families, the worker must respond to the needs of the parents as well as to those of the children. Sometimes, parents can meet the needs of their children only after their own needs have been met. Often parents of children who are deprived of developmental and emotional resources experienced these same lacks in their own upbringing. They may have strengths as adults. They may also yearn for some of the same things their young children do, things which they themselves did not have as children. Thus, the worker may help a mother to find attractive clothing for herself as well as her children. Also, a parent may be much more ready to see her child's need for play after she herself has had a chance to play with the attractive materials the home visitor has brought.

A warning is often given by trainers of people in the "helping" professions — of which child development is a part. They advise workers not to be "too familiar" with clients or patients. Naturally home visitors focus on the requirements of the family they are visiting and do not use the visit as an arena in which to discuss their own home problems. Nor do they constantly insert comments about their own children.

However, impersonal attitudes do not enhance the effectiveness of work done by home visitors. Workers do not have to pretend that they have no life outside their professional activity. This simply makes them seem unreal to the family and reinforces barriers to communication. Every now and then, for example, a worker may feel it appropriate to acknowledge that her child behaved in the same way when he was the age of the parent's child. She may share with an overburdened mother her agreement that the demands of raising a family can be draining. Being friendly, responding warmly, and sharing are qualities of the truly helping person. Home visitors, however, do not use the professional relationship as a sounding board for working out their own personal problems and concerns.

ACTIVITIES OF THE HOME VISITOR

While the specific activities the worker performs in the home may vary according to the purposes of the visit, there seem to be some general areas of activity which home visitors perform. Often an agency or school needs basic observational information on a child and family. The significance of the home environment in the life of the child suggests that the home itself is the place where necessary information to serve the child and family can be gathered. Questions such as the following can be answered: What is the home like physically? What is the climate, or "feeling tone," in the home? How do family members interact with each other? How does the child respond to other people? What does the family do — how do they fill their time? In general, what seems to be the family's strengths and weaknesses? To be a good observer, a visitor keeps eyes and ears open, without prying or seeming to be a "busybody."

Many formal programs whose basis is work with families in the home involve the use of educational and play materials. A worker may have a fund of "activity" skills — ideas for crafts made out of home scraps, knowledge of toys and playthings, and a grasp of practical ways of helping children use material. All of these are most useful for work within the home. Workers may use the playthings with the child and demonstrate their uses. Parents are drawn into using them also so that they will be able to continue involving the child with them after the worker leaves. Use of materials with both parents and children is often a good way to open communication. Mutual involvement in an activity promotes relaxation. Workers may be able to show that playthings and activities not only help children learn, but can also reduce discipline and management problems.

If the purpose of the home visits are to help the parents understand and deal with their child more meaningfully, the worker may be called upon to interpret and describe the child's behavior in developmental terms. Usually this is done within the framework of the worker's understanding of child development and of techniques for young children which can be helpful and supportive to parents. Comments may be based on the visitor's own observations as well as information supplied by parents.

Encouraging parents to be more effective may in many cases involve helping them to feel better about themselves as persons — above and beyond the fact of parenthood. Thus, home visitors may deal with matters pertaining directly to the parents. These may take a variety of forms. A worker may suggest ways for a mother who is "tied down" to find baby-sitters and interesting community activities. New ideas for streamlining housework may be brought up. Description of community resources to help parents with specific problems may be offered.

While some programs for young children have social workers who may assist parents with matters related to their personal lives, many do not. This often means that teachers and others meet this need instead. Often *indigenous paraprofessionals* — persons who live in the same community as the parents — are assigned to work with them. Some feel that such people can be particularly supportive in this way.

PROBLEMS IN HOME VISITING

It is important that home visitors be aware of certain problems which may arise in the course of making visits. This will help visitors to be both comfortable and effective in this important job.

One of the first tasks of home visitors should be to clarify their role and the role of the family in the home visiting process. This can prevent difficulties related to misunderstanding the purposes of the visits or the roles of each party from developing. From the viewpoint of the visitors, this ensures that they recognize that their positions as professional workers do not require that they act like members of the family. While home visitors as previously stated should be warm, genuine, and receptive, they should not interfere in ongoing situations which are unrelated to their reasons for making the visits. From the viewpoint of families, they need to recognize that home visitors should not be expected to perform tasks which one might ask of a friend or relative. For example, home visitors would not answer the phone or "mind the baby for a minute" while his mother "runs around the corner for groceries." Both parties need to bear in mind that even though the visits occur within the greater intimacy of the home setting, the relationship is still a professional one. Possible exceptions would be in the event of a real emergency.

The role of the home visitor is different from that of the homemaker. *Homemakers* are specifically utilized to work with families in need of assistance in running the home. Thus, it is appropriate for homemakers to care for the children, purchase and prepare food, and perform other domestic tasks.

Maintenance of confidentiality is a prime requirement in all professional practice. The safeguarding of the right to privacy should be underscored with reference to home visiting. Home visitors must be scrupulous in taking the greatest care not to reveal information about the family and the visits to people who should not have it. When the home visitor lives in the same neighborhood, the family may be justifiably worried that the visitor may gossip about it to mutual acquaintances or others. The visitor should realize that this concern exists and assure the family that this will not happen — that the strictest confidentiality will be kept.

Section 4 Parent-Teacher Contacts

SUMMARY

Home visits by sensitive workers with a sound understanding of child development as well as ways of working with adults can be extremely effective in supporting the well-being of families and children alike. In recognition of this fact, many programs designed to serve children include provision for work within the home.

There are many advantages to working within the home. Parents feel more relaxed there than they do in offices and may be able to communicate more freely. Workers can show parents positive ways of handling their children instead of just talking to them about it. They have the opportunity to observe the family's strengths as well as weaknesses.

Home visitors need to have special sensitivities. They need to understand the needs of adults whose own childhoods may have been deprived. They need to know how to be warm and supportive within the framework of a professional relationship. It is important for home visitors to be able to accept parents as they are and to move slowly in attempts to change them.

There are several different functions workers may fill in working in the home. These include involving children and parents in activities, discussing the child's development and the personal concerns of parents, and gathering observational information. Home visitors, whose role is different from that of homemakers, must maintain strictest confidentiality about their work with families.

SUGGESTED ACTIVITIES

- Arrange with your supervisor to make a home visit to a child who is attending your school. Perhaps the supervisor can suggest a reason for making the visit: to get more information on the child's home behavior, to meet a child before he starts school, to demonstrate a new plaything. After making the visit, compare your feelings and observations about it with contacts you have had with parents within the school setting.

- You have been assigned to visit the Smith family at home to describe the program of your school. Discuss how you will behave when you arrive at their home and throughout your visit.

- Select a plaything which you feel both a parent and a child would find attractive. What educational and social experiences can it provide? Describe how you might present the plaything when making a home visit and various ways in which it might be helpful to the child and family.

- Discuss the process of home visiting with an experienced home visitor. What is this person's perceptions of the assets of home visiting? What problems does he or she see that the prospective visitor should be alerted to?

- Find a fellow student to work with you. Role play the following situations — with one of you playing a mother and the other a home visitor:
  a. Worker responding when a mother criticizes the school program which the worker is representing.
  b. Mother describing how difficult she finds her day-to-day life with small children.

c. Mother asking worker if she herself has children.
d. Father questioning the need of a child for special help.

List the insights role playing the situation contributed towards your understanding of techniques of working in the home.

REVIEW

A. Briefly answer each of the following.

1. Describe four types of programs which include home visiting as part of their service.
2. List three aspects of home visits which enhance communication between parents and workers.
3. Describe two sensitivities which should be possessed by the home visitor. State why each is important.
4. Describe the role of confidentiality in home visiting.

B. Indicate the best choice for each of the following.

1. Mrs. Green offers her home visitor a piece of cake she has just baked. The visitor's least appropriate response might be

   a. Yes, please, I'd enjoy a piece.
   b. I'm sorry, I don't eat on the job.
   c. It looks so good — but I'm trying to diet.
   d. I'd like the recipe for that.

2. While visiting the Smith house, the worker observes Mrs. Smith slap her toddler, who has just pulled a breakable object off a low table. The worker's best response might be

   a. You're frustrating his autonomy.
   b. I know a good book on toddler development you should read.
   c. It's upsetting when an exploring child breaks things, isn't it?
   d. Oh, my, you mustn't spank him!

3. All of the following activities are appropriate for the child development home visitor to perform except

   a. Discussing household management.
   b. Discussing the worker's marital problems.
   c. Observing the family's interaction.
   d. Involving the parent and child in an activity.

4. Mrs. Johnson, Johnny's mother, tells the home visitor that she is ashamed of her clothing and thus will not attend the school picnic. The worker might best reply

   a. Oh, nobody will notice.
   b. That reminds me — let's discuss Johnny's clothes.
   c. Perhaps we can work together on helping you find a new outfit.
   d. It's very important that Johnny goes to the picnic.

Section 4 Parent-Teacher Contacts

5. The staff of a preschool feels that the Owens family needs to set more limits for their son Jim. The most effective way of helping them do this might be

    a. Have them view a film on discipline.
    b. Make a home visit to the family in which the visitor works with Jim in the parent's presence.
    c. Suggest several good books on child management.
    d. Tell the Owens that they should set more limits for Jim.

6. A mother asks the home visitor whose assignment it is to demonstrate and use play materials, to go to the grocery store for her, in order to save her time because she is going out later. The worker should

    a. Go out to the store.
    b. Tactfully suggest that this is not part of the visitor's role, but acknowledge the mother's wish for help.
    c. Offer to call the store and have groceries delivered.
    d. Tell the mother that she will bring groceries the next time she comes.

Section 5 The Exceptional Child

unit 12 identifying the exceptional child

OBJECTIVES

After studying this unit, the student should be able to
- List and describe different kinds of exceptional children.
- Discuss patterns of attitudes held towards exceptional children.
- Describe particular problems encountered by parents of exceptional children.

There has always been a significant number of children who have shown behavior problems, physical handicaps, and learning difficulties which have sometimes caused problems in handling and programming them. Such children may be referred to as exceptional, atypical, or special children. The term exceptional is perhaps the most commonly used.

For many years, young children who were demonstrating severe problems in growing were not recognized. If they were recognized, in many cases they did not receive appropriate treatment. There were several reasons for this. First, most young children did not come into public view until they entered school, at which time their problems finally came to the attention of authorities. Only then were attempts made to provide special help. Also, there was lack of widespread knowledge about the nature of exceptionality. This was particularly true in the case of very young children. It was felt that they would "grow out of" their difficulties. Finally, there was a lack of organized programs and of methods for helping very young exceptional children. The services that did exist were often beyond the financial reach or physical access of many families.

Over the past few decades, this situation has been changing. Increasing recognition of the significance of the early years of development for all children has taken place. This in turn has increased public awareness of the particular needs of exceptional children. With this and legislative support, exceptional

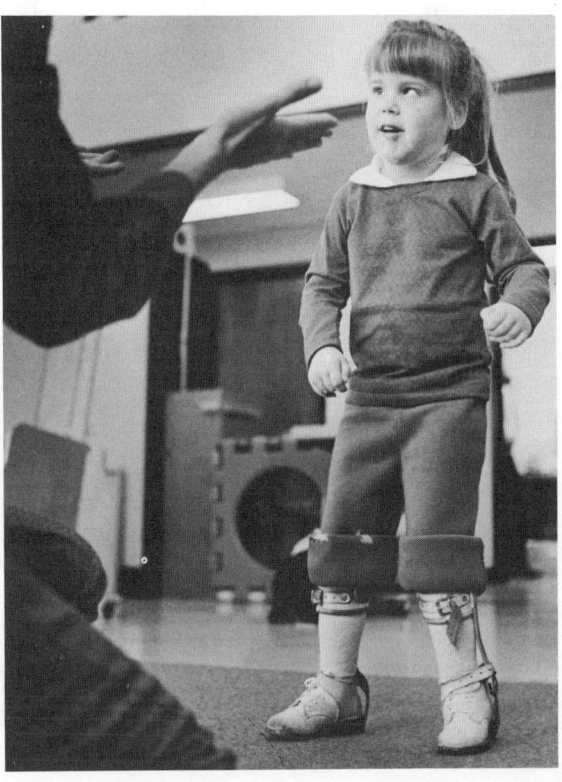

105

children today have a greater probability of having their needs met and of growing to their optimal potential. Because of the surge in activity around development of more programs for exceptional children, it is important that the child care assistant have a strong knowledge base of their particular characteristics and needs, and of the services available for them.

IDENTIFYING EXCEPTIONAL CHILDREN

The assistant working in early childhood programs may encounter children who are "exceptional." The question then arises: "How can one identify such children?" Unless a child's differentiating characteristics are extremely obvious, such as a major physical handicap, the identification of a child with special needs is not always easy.

Several criteria similar to those proposed by Clinebell and Clinebell[1] may help staff know when a child may benefit from additional evaluation or study to determine whether or not his behavior or symptoms fall outside the wide normal range of development for his age. These include (1) timing, (2) frequency, (3) duration (4) intensity, and (5) progression.

By timing is meant the appropriateness of the behavior to the child's stage of development. For example, a two-year-old who eats with his fingers is acting normally. This would have a greatly different meaning for a ten-year-old, however. Similarly, it is well within normal developmental behavior for a three-year-old to want to take a special stuffed animal to school with him as a link to home. Such an activity would hardly be appropriate for a thirteen-year-old. One must be on guard, however, when interpreting norms of behavior, because these are averages — indicating that there is a considerable range in the timing in which an individual child might reach a developmental point.

Frequency refers to how often a certain behavior occurs. If, for example, a four-year-old has a severe temper tantrum — throwing objects and screaming — twice a month, it is not the same as if the child did this five times in one morning.

Duration means how long the symptom or behavior has been present. If a child who has been speaking suddenly stops, this has a different meaning than not talking has in a child who has never spoken. For the child who has suddenly stopped, there may be a specific situational cause. For the child who has never talked, there can be deeper developmental roots.

A child may perform an activity with a reasonable degree of involvement and be able to move away from it to something else in time, if necessary. Another child may react intensely with severe temper tantrums, if someone interferes even slightly with his activity. These are examples of differences in *intensity* of behavior. They have different meanings in terms of determining exceptionality.

Finally, a child's puzzling or troubling behavior can be evaluated from the viewpoint of whether, in general, it is progressively getting worse, staying the same, or improving. Consideration of this factor of *progression* can provide cues as to the need of the child for special help.

In addition to the above cited criteria for studying behavior, the worker should bear in mind the previously described factors of cultural background and basic temperament. The child may be behaving in accordance with the way he has been taught in his particular culture or with his individual behavior style. Here, again it is important to look for extremes.

CATEGORIES OF EXCEPTIONAL CHILDREN

Various diagnostic categories of exceptionality have been proposed. These generally include physically handicapped, mentally

---

[1] Clinebell, C.H., and Clinebell, H.J., *Crisis and Growth: Helping Your Troubled Child.* Philadelphia: Fortress Press, 1971.

retarded, minimally brain damaged and learning disabled, and emotionally disturbed. These categorical descriptions can be helpful in recognizing those specific behaviors or symptoms which might characterize a particular condition. It should be borne in mind, however, that no matter what category a child seems to "fit," he is more a child than "mentally retarded," "emotionally disturbed," or any similiar label. All children — normal and exceptional — have the same basic requirements. All need friends, play, and education. They also all have to deal with the same feelings: anger, anxiety, love, affection, joy, despair. They all must have a positive self-concept derived from nurturing, growth-encouraging care.

Physically Handicapped Children

Physically handicapped children are those who have an impairment of their bodies which affects their ability to interact with the environment. There are a number of physical handicaps which prevent children from having full locomotion, use of their limbs, and muscular control. *Cerebral palsy* is an example of one of these. In this condition, the child has such extremely poor control of his muscles that his movements are uncoordinated. He has difficulty carrying out activities requiring motor precision. *Spina bifida* is another example. Due to a defect in the formation of the spinal column, a child with spina bifida cannot move or control his body below the waist. *Blindness* and *deafness,* which occur both partially and completely, are also physical handicaps. Like the others, they prevent the child from having full sensory contact with the world.

There are those who believe that all children with physical handicaps are not of normal intelligence. While sometimes the biological factors which cause a physical handicap may also affect the child's intellectual ability, this is by no means always the case. In addition, it is particularly difficult to assess a child's cognitive potential when a handicap may have interfered with his ability to have the interaction with the environment which contributes towards intellectual competence.

Mentally Retarded Children

Mentally retarded children are those whose primary handicap is intellectual. Their capacity for learning is below that of the general population. There is a great degree of variation in the amount of retardation children may demonstrate. For some children, retardation appears only in their academic performance in school. They otherwise lead completely normal lives. On the other extreme are children who never develop mentally beyond infancy. These profoundly retarded individuals may never speak, sit up, or walk; they require special care all their lives. Among the known causes of retardation are those which are physical in nature. Gross damage to the brain and genetic causes, such as in the case of *Down's Syndrome,* are among these. Down's Syndrome is commonly known as mongolism. Children who have it show distinct physical characteristics, such as slitted eyes. Mongoloid children have distinct individual personalities and a wide range of mental ability, ranging from profound to only moderate retardation.

There seems to be evidence that some retarded functioning in children is related to early deprivation and lack of stimulation. Children who have experienced neglect or abuse or have experienced many changes in caretaker, may appear to be retarded by demonstrating developmental lags and unusual behavior. *Failure to thrive* children — infants who do not seem to be developing physically, even though there is no apparent cause — may fall into the category of those experiencing social, emotional, and cognitive deprivation. This seems to affect the very basis of their functioning. With many children, the introduction of a more stable and stimulating environment, with consistent and attentive care, can set development on a positive track. Some of these children have made exceptional gains under such circumstances.

Brain Damaged Children

Brain damaged children are those who, as the term suggests, have suffered some organic damage to their brain. The behavioral characteristics of brain damaged children may include distractibility, short attention span, impulsiveness, inability to postpone gratification, aggression, destructiveness, poor motor coordination, and the inability to recognize or manipulate symbols. Children who demonstrate some of these behaviors in the absence of proved brain damage are sometimes referred to as *minimally brain damaged*. The assumption is that there must be some brain pathology causing the behavior. Other terms have been applied to children displaying some of these behavioral characteristics. One is *hyperactive* or *hyperkinetic* to describe those who are particularly active and impulsive. Others are *perceptually-motor handicapped* and *learning disabled* to designate those with problems in coordination and ability to use symbols.

Many brain damaged, minimally brain damaged, hyperkinetic, and perceptually motor handicapped children are of normal or potentially normal intelligence. Some are very bright. Their disorganized behavior and inability to organize stimuli make it difficult for them to learn and to behave appropriately in academic settings without special care, however.

Emotionally Disturbed Children

Emotionally disturbed children are those who have difficulty handling their feelings and in behaving in a manner appropriate to their age. There may or may not be a physical basis for their condition. Some physically handicapped, mentally retarded, and minimally brain damaged children develop emotional problems as a result of experiencing the original handicap. Emotional disturbance may be present when behaviors are displayed to excess — beyond the wide range which encompasses normality. These behaviors include aggressiveness, anxiety, withdrawal, apathy, fearfulness, inability to play, repetitive activity, inability to tolerate change, habit disturbances (such as eating and sleeping problems), disinterest in people, communication and language difficulties, and physical mannerisms which lack a demonstrable organic basis.

Among the most profound emotional disturbances in young children are the *childhood psychoses*. Psychoses are suggested by children's inability to relate to reality and highly bizarre behavior. Early infantile autism is another severe emotional disturbance. *Autism* is characterized by the desire of the child to preserve sameness and by a failure to respond to people. Autistic children become very upset if they observe any change in their physical surroundings. They may tend to respond to people as objects rather than as persons. There is controversy as to whether autism has a physical or psychological cause. Autistic children are felt to be of potentially normal intelligence, however, and respond to special therapeutic approaches.

ATTITUDES TOWARDS EXCEPTIONAL CHILDREN

As has been stated, there is a growing acceptance of exceptionality in children. There are still public attitudes which can hinder the advancement of these children with special needs, however.

Some people believe that while exceptional children should be helped, they should be hidden away from other children so that their characteristics do not affect "normal" children. Such children, they feel, should be "put away" as if they did not exist. Fortunately, the number who feel this way is diminishing.

There are others who feel that while exceptional children should be helped, there should be a limit to the amount of special programming provided for severely handicapped children. Since, they feel, these children may never reach the same capacity as essentially normal children, too many resources should not be expended on them.

One attitude appears on the surface to be constructive, but is subtly undermining to the welfare of handicapped and exceptional children. This is the feeling that they should be pitied and kept dependent. This attitude results in the holding out of insufficient expectations for the children, which further impairs their development. For example, a well-meaning person may dress or feed an exceptional child when the most helpful approach is to help him learn to do these things himself. Attitudes of pity not only detract from the possibility of the child achieving his true potential, but also rob him of his self-esteem and sense of dignity.

ATTITUDES TOWARDS PARENTS OF EXCEPTIONAL CHILDREN

Closely related to general public attitudes towards exceptionality are the attitudes held towards parents of exceptional children and the attitudes that the parents themselves may develop.

It is difficult for parents of normal children and professionals who have contact with exceptional children only during a working day to recognize the impact on parents of having an exceptional child. Professional persons need to be sensitive to the feelings of parents if their work with the whole family is to be effective.

Frequently parents of exceptional children carry a tremendous load of guilt feelings. They may feel that somehow they did something to cause the child's handicap. This is particularly true in the case of emotionally disturbed children in which origins may not be physically demonstrated. A mother may feel, for example, that if she had taken better care of herself during pregnancy, she would not have had a retarded child. Another mother may feel that if she had not left her infant overnight with baby-sitters several times, he would not now be emotionally disturbed.

Effects of these guilt feelings can be harmful to all concerned. Parents may overprotect a handicapped child, thereby restricting his opportunity for further development. They do not want to risk having to experience further guilt by letting the child try anything that has the slightest possibility of danger. Or, the parents may "spoil" the exceptional child, wanting to make up to him through overindulgence what they think they have done to him. The child is not expected to try to behave and is generally favored. This is particularly difficult for other children in the family. They may come to feel deprived and develop feelings of resentment for their exceptional sibling.

Living with some exceptional children, no matter how much they are loved, can be difficult for other family members. Autistic or hyperactive children can constantly upset a household with their uncontrolled activity. They require constant supervision. Sometimes nobody will baby-sit with such a child, and the parents cannot go out together or otherwise have a break from the child's demands. The exceptional child may destroy siblings' toys or interrupt their play with friends.

Unfortunately, the exhaustion and exasperation which has sometimes been observed in parents may be interpreted as rejection of the children. Rather, it may be a normal response to the strain of around-the-clock living with them.

In some families, the marital relationship has been negatively affected by the advent of an exceptional child. Husband and wife may blame each other for the child's problems. Disagreements over major planning for the child may occur. One parent may wish to keep a child at home; the other, to institutionalize him. Financial problems resulting from payments for special care may contribute towards family stress and tension.

Those working with exceptional children should also recognize ways in which such a child contributes to family strength and solidarity. Parenting an exceptional child frequently brings out the highest qualities of optimism and devotion. Siblings and their friends often learn compassion and caring through interaction with the exceptional child. In fortunate cases, planning for and working with the child have not only drawn parents together, but have involved neighbors, also. Growth and new achievements of the child, such as reaching an academic milestone, can bring the entire family special feelings of pride.

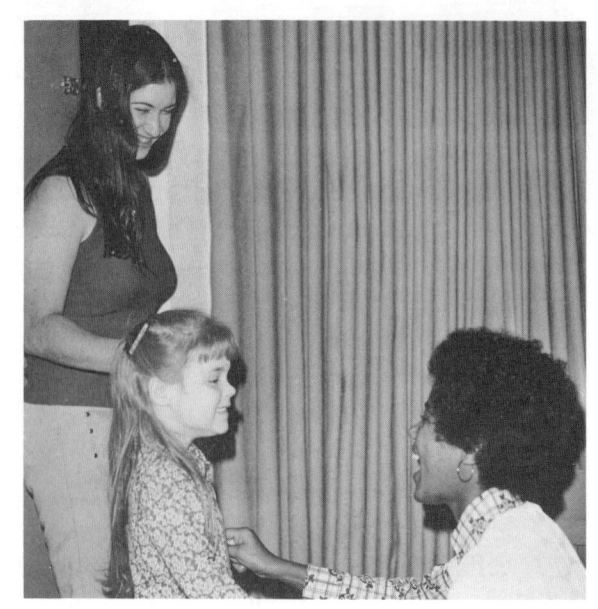

SUMMARY

In recent years, there has been increasing recognition of the needs of exceptional children who may be mentally retarded, physically handicapped, brain damaged, or emotionally disturbed. Such children are still more like all children than like the specific diagnostic category which may have been applied to them, however.

While public attitudes towards exceptional children have improved, there are still those who believe these children should be "put away" or pitied. Professionals must be sensitive to both the difficulties and assets of parents living with exceptional children.

SUGGESTED ACTIVITIES

- Observe a child who has been identified as belonging to one of the described categories of exceptionality. What impact does his handicap seem to have on his ability to interact with the environment? How do you think this has affected his overall development?

- Observe a group which includes, or is made up of, exceptional children. In what ways are they similar to normal children? How are they different?
- Talk to several people informally about their attitudes towards exceptional and handicapped children. How do their comments compare with the kinds of attitudes described in the text?
- Make a home visit to a family in which there is a severely handicapped or disturbed child. In what ways has the child had an impact on ongoing family life? What positive effects can be seen?
- Read *This Stranger My Son* by Louise Brown (G.P. Putnam, 1968) or *Our Son, Ken* by Sarah E. Lorenz (Dell, 1969). Both are parent's accounts of raising emotionally disturbed children. Would you have behaved differently from these parents in handling the children? Did these readings influence your attitudes towards parents? What are the implications of these accounts for persons working professionally with children and their families?

REVIEW

A. Define each of the following.

    1. Spina bifida

    2. Autism

    3. Minimal brain damage

B. Indicate the best choice for each of the following.

    1. Children who do not seem to develop physically with no organic basis are considered

        a. Hyperkinetic.   c. Autistic.
        b. Failure to thrive.   d. Aphasic.

    2. Johnny likes to sit and spin a top for hours on end. When he enters his room at home, he quickly changes back any furniture which has been moved. When he wants something, he takes the hand of an adult and pulls him towards the object. Johnny has symptoms characteristic of

        a. Cerebral palsy.   c. Autism
        b. Childhood psychosis.   d. Minimal brain damage.

    3. Jim gets along well with neighbors and friends and has an after school job in a grocery store. He is sixteen and in the seventh grade. Jane is five, cannot sit up, is fed with a bottle, and spends most of her time in a crib. Both of these children might be called

        a. Different.   c. Mentally retarded.
        b. Emotionally disturbed.   d. Hyperactive.

Section 5 The Exceptional Child

        4. Exceptional children
           a. Only need love in order to thrive.
           b. Are always rejected by their parents.
           c. Have mannerisms which "rub off" on normal children.
           d. Should have reasonable expectations set for them.

C. List and define four criteria for helping to determine if a child's behavior may require special evaluation and help.

unit 13   the exceptional child in class and community

OBJECTIVES

After studying this unit, the student should be able to

- Describe issues in programming for exceptional children: home vs. institutional care; stigma and labeling; mainstreaming and normalization.
- Discuss the dynamics of integrating the exceptional child into the classroom.
- List and define models of community and service programs for exceptional young children.

One of the most heartrending and difficult decisions facing any parent of a moderately or severely handicapped child is whether to keep the child at home or to institutionalize him. It is generally recommended that families seek expert counseling so that they understand the complexities involved before taking action.

HOME VS INSTITUTIONAL CARE

There seems to be considerable evidence that young children, even those with severe deficiencies, make much greater developmental progress when raised in a family instead of an institutional setting. Some feel that institutionalization is only appropriate for those children who are so impaired that they need intensive, around-the-clock, specialized medical attention.

Several factors can enter into the decision of whether or not to send a child to a public institution. One of these is the family's resources. One family may have access to appropriate community programs and sufficient income to pay for specialized care and help. Another family may not have these supports. The number of other children in the family is another variable. Naturally, the quality of care provided in the institution is a major consideration. A large, distant "custodial" institution is likely to have a different effect on a child than a small one which is nearby and has developmental programming and provision for individual attention.

Today, fortunately, parents are less likely to be confronted with this difficult decision. With the trend towards developing community based care for people with special needs and providing increased subsidy for such programs, a greater number of handicapped children can remain at home while receiving appropriate services.

STIGMA AND LABELING

Some people feel that there is an unfortunate by-product of programs which only enroll exceptional children, valuable as these programs can be. The process of selecting children for such programs has involved diagnosis, or the determination of a category of disorder into which the child's symptoms would seem to fit. This has necessarily required labeling the child as "mentally retarded," "emotionally disturbed," or a similar category. While such assignment of diagnostic labels may be necessary in order to develop a program for the child, it is suggested that the process of labeling can have some less positive effects. These revolve around *stigmatization* — the assignment of negative stereotypes. By tending to "box" children in categories, labels set up expectations that the children will always behave in the manner implied by the labels. The child's own perception of the label applied to him may have destructive effects on his self-concept. If a child knows that he has the stigma of being called retarded, he may feel that it is no use to try to grow and change.

Increasing recognition of the negative effects which can occur as a result of labeling — which are reinforced when children in similar diagnostic categories are grouped together — is now taking place. As a result, there is a growing trend towards including exceptional children in programs for normal children.

MAINSTREAMING AND NORMALIZATION

The growing practice of decreasing segregation through enrolling handicapped children in regular programs is called *mainstreaming*. Perhaps a major advantage of mainstreaming is its relationship to a new concept which is radically changing the provision of services to people who have been considered "different." This is the concept of *normalization* developed by Wolf Wolfensberger.[1] Essentially, this means that all activities provided for persons considered different should encourage their functioning as much as possible as other persons in the community do. This is in contrast to having deviancy reinforced by attitudes and practices which segregate and dehumanize.

Wolfensberger feels that mainstreaming is a normalizing practice. In fact, he feels it is particularly appropriate for young children who, having not yet had the opportunity to develop negative attitudes towards differences, can accommodate to them most adequately.

[1] W. Wolfensberger. *The Principle of Normalization in Human Services.* Toronto: National Institute on Mental Retardation, 1972.

There is considerable evidence that mainstreaming can have many positive benefits for all. For the exceptional children, models of normal behavior are provided in an atmosphere in which such behavior is automatically expected and encouraged. The type of programming offered is likely to appeal to the children's strengths, as well as to their weaknesses. Interaction with other children stimulates their social and cognitive development. The normal children learn to understand and interact on a daily basis with children with special problems. This can contribute towards the development of positive attitudes and new ways of caring for others.

THE EXCEPTIONAL CHILD IN THE CLASSROOM

There are guidelines which can be used to help the effective integration of exceptional children in regular programs. It should be recognized that special attention may have to be given to physical factors involving space and safety. Staff need to work closely together to develop an environment that is positive for all. A physically handicapped child may have to have a special piece of equipment in the classroom with him. The staff will need to locate an appropriate place for it.

There may be special instructions for the exceptional child which may have been established by the agency which referred the child to the program. It may have been recommended that the child be encouraged to fasten his own clothing, begin to use regular utensils, or crawl on a mat. It is important that the work with the children be coordinated by the staff so the children can experience reinforcement, rather than fragmentation.

The point was previously made that exceptional children are more like children than like any diagnostic label which may have been used to describe them. As many of their characteristics are similar to those of other youngsters, they can often be treated in similar ways.

In fact, it is frequently emphasized that the developmental goals of well-run preschool programs are highly suitable for exceptional children — provided that they, along with each other child in the program, are regarded as individuals as well. All children need to learn to understand their feelings, to relate to other people, to manipulate objects and symbols, and to have positive feelings about themselves. Appropriately guided play and educational and social experiences provided by caring staff will contribute towards their achieving these goals.

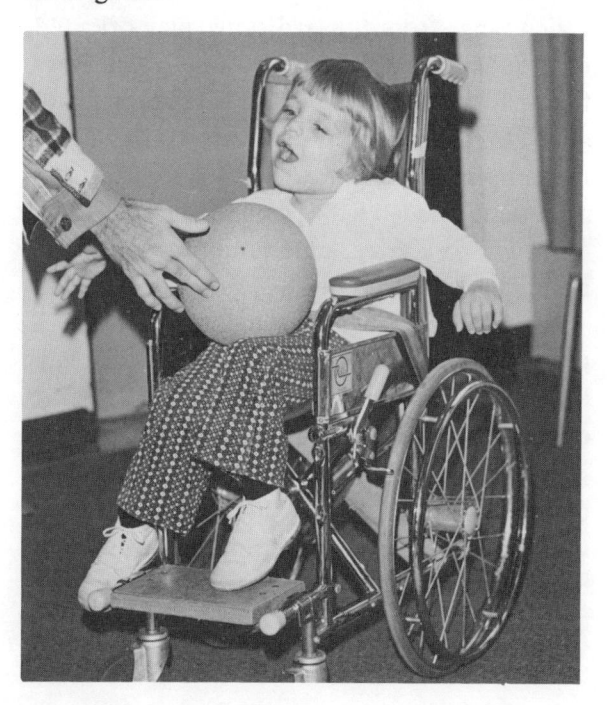

DYNAMICS OF INTEGRATION

Even though it has been stated that exceptional children in many ways can be handled as normal children are, this may be difficult for some staff to do, particularly at first. When a child has been diagnosed as having some kind of special problem, the staff may be fearful about the child. They may wonder if he will be safe, if the other children will make awkward comments, if they as teachers might expect either too much or too little.

Careful preparation for the advent of the child should help to prevent this fear. If, for example, staff knows exactly what the capacities of a physically handicapped child are, that knowledge should help them handle him appropriately.

Adults may bring their own childhood attitudes towards exceptionality into the classroom. Staff who feel that the handicapped child is simply to be pitied, or "only needs love," may provide him insufficient encouragement to join activities. They may tolerate behavior which is actually within the child's ability to control. This neither promotes growth in the exceptional child, nor encourages positive responses towards him from the other children. These children may resent the failure of staff to place reasonable limits on their classmate. It is also important that there is sufficient staff so that all children receive appropriate attention.

Sometimes, a staff member may identify too closely with an exceptional child, feeling that only she can give the child the special understanding that he needs. This *rescue fantasy* — conviction that a child's salvation lies in one's hands — often results in the staff member becoming overly involved and overprotective. She may focus on the one child only, rather than on the group as a whole. As a result, the other children are neglected, the exceptional child is not encouraged to be a group member, and other personnel become resentful. In addition, the deeply involved staff member may be jealous of other adults' relationships with the child, which further contributes to staff unrest.

This does not mean that the exceptional child, like the other children, should not be given individual consideration. Special attention should be provided in a way that is directed towards helping him to be a part of the group, rather than an isolate within it. As with all children, it is important that the atypical child be given the opportunity to experience success.

It is true that sometimes a severely handicapped child really needs a "special" staff member so that he can have the guidance necessary for him to join the program. In this way, he is less apt to disrupt the others and will receive appropriate support which may contribute to his positive participation in the program. When carefully implemented, this can be an effective plan. Discussion with the other children and staff concerning the one child's need for a special worker can head off feelings of jealousy and resentment.

As staff working in an integrated classroom gradually see the progress of the exceptional child and the growth in understanding of the other children, they experience a justifiable feeling of gratification. This is most important and gives a sense of self-esteem which can contribute towards increasing professional commitment and development.

It can be expected that a growing number of regular programs will integrate exceptional children. Some must already do so by legislative mandate. For example, a 1972 amendment to the Head Start legislation required that at least 10 percent of the places in Head Start be allocated to handicapped children.

MODELS OF COMMUNITY AND SERVICE PROGRAMS FOR EXCEPTIONAL CHILDREN

There are many contemporary service models for exceptional children. *Special education* programs are presently conducted for many kinds of exceptional children — blind, physically handicapped, retarded. Many of these are similar in organization and focus to the interventive programs described in earlier units. They stress prevention rather than remediation. It is felt that the earlier the intervention occurs, the more effective it will be in helping handicapped children reach their full potential. Today there are program models serving infants and toddlers as well as preschool children. Curricula are utilized which range from the traditional play-oriented to the highly structured and cognitively focused. An example of an educational program for exceptional children is the *Early Education Project for Multihandicapped Children* conducted by the United Cerebral Palsy of New York City, under support from the Handicapped Children's Early Education Assistance Act. This program includes a physical environment similar to that of regular preschools, individualized curricula, play opportunities, and work with families.[2]

The *therapeutic preschool* is a fairly recent educational model for young children with developmental and emotional problems. Such schools may appear physically very

---

[2] Berta Rafael "Early Education for Multihandicapped Children." *Children Today,* Jan.- Feb. 1973, pp. 22-26.

much like regular preschool classrooms. However, the staff is usually especially trained to understand and work with this particular type of child. Special attention is given to recognizing and responding to the children's communications and to facilitating positive group relationships. The children are helped to gain a sense of mastery of their feelings and the environment. The staff provides images of adults who are caring and trustworthy. Therapeutic preschools frequently employ psychological or psychiatric consultation to assist the staff in working with the children.

Diagnostic clinics and programs exist as an essential means for precisely identifying the nature of problems in children who apparently are handicapped. Sometimes diagnostic work is done by specialists in private practice. Institutional programs such as hospitals and community mental health centers may also conduct diagnostic programs. They may utilize the expertise of a variety of professionals: pediatricians, social workers, child development and child care specialists, psychiatrists, psychologists, speech therapists, and others. These professionals gather all information relevant to the child's history and current functioning, carefully observe and study the child, and arrive at a diagnosis and a suggested plan of treatment through pooling and integrating their specialized information.

Residential centers and institutions provide twenty-four hour a day live-in care for children whose needs apparently cannot be met in their own homes and communities. They operate under both public and private sponsorship. Ideally, such settings attempt to provide an environment in which daily routines and activities are designed to help the child develop so that he can eventually return home. As was previously mentioned, however, such settings often do not have adequate resources. Thus, the children's needs for food and shelter may be met in a custodial fashion. They may fail to serve a truly interventive function which can only be accomplished through specialized services.

Community mental health programs reflect the trend away from large institutional programs and toward providing care for both adults and children with special problems in their own community. Community mental health programs are structured to give a variety of services to persons residing in a given geographical area. Their programs may include therapeutic groups, parent education, family counseling, individual treatment, assistance in utilizing other community resources, and hospitalization.

Private practitioners provide service on an individual fee basis, rather than as salaried employees of an agency. These specialists include psychiatrists, psychologists, and social workers. *Psychiatrists* are medical doctors with special training in psychodynamics. They have particular skill, therefore, in evaluating problems in which there may be physical involvement. *Psychologists* are experts in testing and diagnosis, as well as in various therapeutic approaches. *Social workers* are oriented towards relationships in their social context. Social workers may work with a child's family helping them to better understand and handle him and with community agencies which can also give helpful service to the family.

A growing profession is that of child development and child care specialists. These are individuals with special skills in direct work with children, who use their knowledge of both normal and exceptional development to help children increase their social, emotional, and cognitive abilities. Special education teachers may sometimes work individually with exceptional children, usually as tutors.

Parental support systems have recently been developing to help parents of exceptional children better meet both their own and the children's needs. Parent groups, organized around a specific handicap, have been formed and have made some important achievements. Some of them have succeeded in having legislation passed to provide more services. For example, the Right to Education Act, mandating that public schools supply education for retarded children, was the result of action initiated by the Pennsylvania Association for Retarded Children.

Discussion groups have permitted parents to share experiences and ideas for more effectively living with their children. Participants found that simply knowing that others have the same kinds of problems has been tremendously supportive. Parents in such groups may also help each other by giving substitute care to each others' children. This provides some relief from the demands of constantly being with the children. The Magazine *The Exceptional Parent* giving guidelines and providing a supportive forum, is also helpful.

SUMMARY

One of the most difficult decisions for parents of exceptional children to make is whether to keep the child at home or to institutionalize him. Many issues are involved, and specialized counseling is recommended before a decision is made.

Because segregation of exceptional children into special programs has resulted in stigmatization, there is a growing trend towards the integration of exceptional children into regular programs, a process called mainstreaming. With appropriate orientation of staff and the other children, this can be quite successful, particularly since the development needs of exceptional children can be effectively met within the program and curricular structure of such settings.

Other service models for exceptional children include special education programs, community mental health programs, diagnostic centers, private practitioners, and parental support systems.

SUGGESTED ACTIVITIES

- Find out what kinds of programming are available for exceptional children in your community. Are these programs similar to the models described in the text?
- Arrange to visit several of your community programs, if possible. How is the children's behavior similar to that of normal children? How is it different? How are program content and organization similar to regular programs you have observed? What concessions have been made to the children's special needs?
- Visit a diagnostic clinic. What kinds of professional disciplines are represented? How do they work together?
- Visit a program which "mainstreams." How do the exceptional children function with the normal children? How does the staff seem to feel about the presence of the exceptional children?

REVIEW

A. Define each of the following.
   1. Normalization
   2. Mainstreaming
   3. Rescue fantasy
   4. Stigma
   5. Child development specialist

B. Indicate the best choice for each of the following.
   1. Which of the following is not a true statement about residential programs?
      a. They should be utilized for all handicapped children.
      b. They may have a different effect on children depending on nearness to the children's homes.
      c. They may vary in quality of care provided.
      d. They may be necessary for children requiring intensive and specialized care.
   2. The professional discipline with special skills in testing and diagnosis of ability and emotional development is
      a. Psychiatry.   c. Psychology.
      b. Social work.   d. Nursing.

C. Briefly answer each of the following.
   1. Describe some of the interpersonal situations which can occur between staff members in relationship to an exceptional child in the classroom group. Discuss ways to prevent them.
   2. Discuss some of the issues confronting parents in planning home or institutional care for children with handicaps.
   3. Compare the therapeutic preschool model with that of a special education program.

Section 6 Community Relationships

unit 14   program resources and the community

OBJECTIVES

After studying this unit, the student should be able to

- Describe the relationship of child care programs to the professional community.
- Describe the relationship of child care programs to the general community.
- List and define sources of community support for programs.

A child care program does not exist apart from the community in which it makes its home. Hopefully, it has been designed to meet the needs of the people who live there and who use its services.

Child care programs rely on the surrounding community for the contribution of resources which help to sustain and improve them. Thus, those who are in the programs wish to maintain positive relationships with professional colleagues in similar and related activities, as well as with the general public. The opinions of these people regarding the value and reputation of the program are important. Positive interaction with them and utilization of their resources play important roles in assuring the overall quality and service of the program.

RELATIONSHIP TO THE PROFESSIONAL COMMUNITY

The professional community relevant to child care programs consists of people who are specifically trained to work with children. These are persons with expertise gained through both education and experience in similar or related programs.

Consultation

One way in which child care programs utilize external professional expertise is through consultation. Frequently child care programs need the advice of a consultant — an expert who is not administratively related to the program. The consultant's function is to suggest ways of improving selected aspects of the operation of the program. Consultation may occur through several means. It may be voluntarily solicited by the director of a program to address specific problems, or by the Board of Directors to examine the total operation of the center. Sometimes, the requirements of the agency funding the program mandate the inclusion of consultation.

Gerald Caplan has helped articulate the structure of consultation; it can take several forms in early childhood programs. One type is in-depth study of individual children. This may involve use of methods which might not be available for use by regular staff through lack of time or educational preparation. This information, along with that contributed by staff from their experience, can be useful. It can increase understanding of a child and suggest appropriate ways of working with him.

Another form of consultation focuses on the programmatic aspects of the agency. The consultant addressing himself to this area may suggest different classroom physical arrangements, curriculum models, teaching strategies, or selection of materials.

Administrative consultation considers the managerial functioning of the agency. This includes such factors as ways of utilizing staff, developing resources, upgrading accounting procedures, and others which can make operation of the agency more efficient and effective in meeting its goals.

The manner in which consultative services are delivered includes observation by the consultant, participation in staff meetings, individual conferences with the director and other staff, and involvement with inservice training programs. *Inservice training* refers to on-the-job education so that staff continually upgrades the quality of its performance. Consultants often provide input into the design and conduct of inservice sessions.

Consultation can make valuable contributions to a program, giving an objective point of view on important problems and concerns. The "outsider" position of the consultant helps him see aspects which may not be as apparent to those with daily involvement in the program. With access to consultation, an agency can receive the benefits without having to carry an additional full time staff member. It should be pointed out, however, that substantial fees are frequently involved in paying consultants. In order for consultation to be as effective as possible, it is important that consumers are sensitive to interpersonal dynamics which can develop around consultation and diminish its impact if not appropriately handled.

Consultants are not administratively attached to programs. That is, they do not carry responsibility for directly providing service. Therefore, the agency has the option of either implementing or rejecting the consultant's suggestions. Naturally, if his advice is consistently ignored, the time spent by all engaged in the consultative process has been wasted. Sometimes staff feels threatened by the consultant. They resent the possibility of an outsider "coming in to criticize us and tell us what to do." Consultation implies some evaluation of the way a program is conducted. Such scrutiny can make even the most flexible and constructive people feel uncomfortable. They may either actively or passively resist acting on the consultant's ideas.

This position is also difficult for the consultant. If he is too fast and too direct in his approach, he runs the risk of being shut out by the staff. On the other hand, if he is too passive or indefinite, the staff then question his competence to react to their program.

One way to reduce staff resistance to consultation is for those who engage the service to clarify for the staff exactly what the role and function of the consultant will be. It is a well-known principle of human interaction that when people do not know what is taking place, they form their own ideas — ideas which may be highly exaggerated. If staff is helped to recognize the supportive and nonadministrative structuring of consultation, they are less likely to resist it. This in turn helps the consultant to be effective, since he can be more open with people.

Training

Child care programs frequently have some type of relationship with training programs preparing people to work professionally with children. Consultants may be faculty members of the sponsoring colleges and universities. These training sites may serve as resource centers for local programs. Frequently they operate their own child care programs as research and demonstration centers and as places in which students can gain direct work experience under supervision.

One of the most frequent links between child care programs and educational institutions involves their collaboration in the training of students. Even if the institution conducts its own program, there are frequently more students needing direct line experience than can be accommodated. Thus, community child care programs provide this essential educational component by permitting students, under supervision, to participate in work with young children.

The educational institution will sometimes pay the agency for their role in providing "field work" for its students. It may, for example, perhaps permit agency staff to enroll in courses without paying tuition. Some agencies and educational programs develop a mutually compatible relationship without formal compensation being made. For the agency, serving as a training site encourages it to keep up-to-date with advances in the field. Many programs which work with students indicate that they find it stimulating to have input from students and contact with supervising faculty. Personnel of such programs also state that they enjoy knowing that they are contributing towards the development of future practitioners. In addition, advanced students may actually provide valuable service to the programs in which they are doing their field work.

It is important that the centers serving as training sites and the educational institutions sponsoring students maintain close and open communication. This ensures mutual understanding as to the functions the students are to perform and the objectives they are to achieve. It is particularly important that adequate provision for student supervision is made, if the training experience is to be successful for all concerned. Students usually participate willingly and helpfully in all aspects of the program as long as they receive adequate orientation, guidelines and directions, and the opportunity to discuss their questions and concerns.

Referrals

A mutual referral system makes up another form of interaction between child care programs and the professional community of practitioners in the field. When these people — pediatricians, therapists in private practice, staff of various human service agencies — recognize that a center offers a sound program, they may wish to refer clients to it. For example, a pediatrician may suggest to a tired mother of an active four-year-old that a preschool experience might be most helpful to both of them. A clinician doing individual play therapy with a child might feel that a group experience would provide further assistance in resolving the child's problems. Conversely, child care personnel may wish to refer specific children and families to appropriate community practitioners. A teacher might wish to recommend to a parent that a child having particular difficulty in the group be examined by a clinical specialist.

RELATIONSHIPS WITH THE GENERAL COMMUNITY

The relationship of a child care program with the general population of the community in which it is located and which it is designed to serve can take several forms.

Preliminary Relationships

Child care centers wishing to establish positive relationships with the surrounding community begin even before opening a contemplated program. Contribution is thus made towards a climate of acceptance before a child ever comes through the door.

Needs Assessment

A prospective program should determine the need for its services before it proceeds with implementation. *Needs assessment* can be conducted in several ways. One is to consult with programs which are already operational in the area to see whether another similar — or different — service is needed. A community mental health program is often in a good position to give such information. Some communities have agencies whose function is to help programs coordinate their efforts so that needed services are provided without unnecessary duplication. These agencies may have access to statistical reports, legislative information, and other concrete data which helps in sound decision making. Another way of acquiring information about community needs is to canvass neighborhood and community groups. For example, church organizations and women's clubs could indicate the needs of membership for child care programs.

It is also helpful to involve key community leaders, or representatives of the population a program might serve, in the planning and implementation process. These groups may have many helpful suggestions. In addition, their participation from the beginning will be more likely to increase their support. It also may decrease the probability that there will be hostility or resistance once the program is begun.

Recruitment

For a program to be able to open and operate, it must have clients or consumers. Recruitment efforts must be made to ensure that an initial and ongoing enrollment is maintained. If community leaders have been contacted, they may help to inform others that a new service is available.

Some programs, once staff is on board and the physical setting is ready to accommodate children, hold an "Open House." Interested individuals can become acquainted with the prospective center by observing and asking questions at this time.

Use of the mass media is also helpful in developing public awareness. A newspaper may do a feature on a new program. Staff members may be able to arrange to appear on a television talk show serving the local area.

Shopping centers, supermarkets, and laundromats are suitable places for posting notices about program openings where they are apt to be seen by potential consumers. Announcements can be sent to the professional community. Speaker's bureaus may list appropriate staff members who can address interested groups on the work of their program.

If there is a local human service coordinating agency, it is important that the new program inform it of its availability. Often,

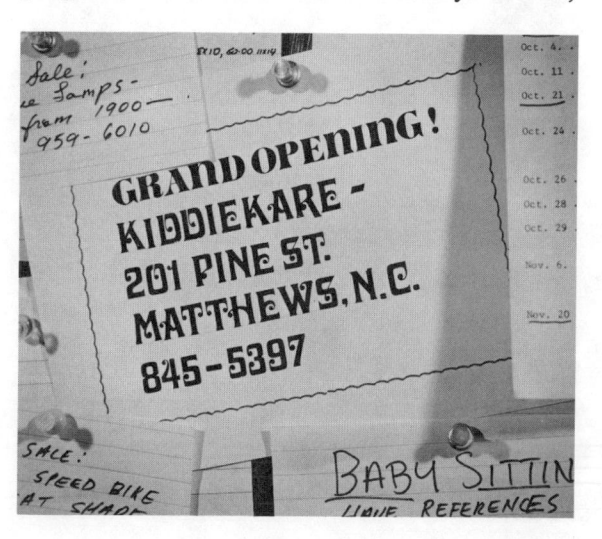

Section 6 Community Relationships

if a program is opened in conjunction with, or under the sponsorship of, a larger organization, people who are involved with the larger unit may utilize the new program as they become aware of it.

Once a program is well under way, "word of mouth" endorsement by satisfied consumers contributes towards continued enrollment and decreases the necessity for active recruitment efforts.

Utilization of Community Resources

Frequently, the income of a child care program is not completely adequate to pay the cost of the program. Then the staff, building upon good community relationships, must turn to sources outside the program for support to augment tuition and other fees it collects.

Fund Raising

Naturally, additional cash is often the type of supplemental resource required by a program. Usually, the board of directors or the director, as part of his administrative function, has the responsibility for seeking external funding.

There is a variety of fund raising methods. One of these is *individual solicitation*. People associated with the program may prepare a list of prominent individuals who have an interest in such services. Then, they may speak with them about the possibility of their making donations.

Foundations comprise another funding source. A foundation is an organization with funds which it wishes to allocate in support of specific problems which it feels are important. They have a tradition of supporting human service activities such as education, medicine, and mental health. If a program wishes to solicit support from a foundation, it prepares a *proposal* to submit to it. A proposal is a detailed statement of the services it intends to provide, the budget necessary for this, and the objectives or goals it wishes to achieve. If the foundation funds a program, it expects that the money will be used in the way originally proposed and that the purposes of the program will be accomplished. Often, foundations only wish to supply "seed" money — funds necessary to get the new program started. The money is given with the expectation that

When it is used up, the program will be self-supporting.

Federal and state governmental agencies (described in more detail in the following unit) are another source of external funding similar in structure and mode of operation to foundations. One of the major differences between the two is that foundations operate within the private, rather than the public, sector.

Community organizations and charities may decide to provide financial assistance to child care programs. For example, the Community Chest, Junior League, or Jaycees may agree to conduct fund raising activities on behalf of a child care program.

Materials Donations

Community resources are sometimes given through donations of materials, rather than money. Often, a church or similar organization provides the physical space for a program, with minimal or no rent. Clubs such as sororities, fraternities, and women's groups may collect and donate materials and equipment. Frequently, such organizations are seeking appropriate targets for holiday donations. Careful searches by staff may locate companies which have scrap materials remaining after manufacture of their product which can be a source of interesting and stimulating materials for children. Such materials might include rug scraps, wood scraps, linoleum and tile pieces, and similar items. Most such companies will save these materials if they are made aware of an interest in them. Program staff may pick up the materials periodically.

Volunteers

A most important and valuable "human" community resource for child care programs are volunteers. Carefully selected and integrated into a program, volunteers can make a substantial contribution. As with participating parents, they can bring special talents to the program which provide additional enrichment. They may also help to perform administrative functions which help the program run smoothly. Children requiring special attention to participate in group activities may be assigned to volunteers.

There are, however, several guidelines for the effective utilization of volunteers. First of all, they should be carefully oriented to their work. They should know the philosophy of the program and ways to appropriately handle young children. The latter is particularly important. Some volunteers may have a tendency to be too rigid, based on the feeling, "I raised my children this way." Others may be inclined to hold too low expectations for the children, feeling that they only "need to be loved." Volunteers should not be randomly "dumped" on a program. They should be carefully assigned roles in accordance with their particular interests and assets.

Staff need to understand their relationship with volunteers. This will ensure that they do not feel threatened by them or that their jobs will be taken from them. Some staff believe that volunteers do not understand what they are doing and may misrepresent them in the community.

In order to prevent problems arising from the use of volunteers, and because they wish to gain the greatest benefits from volunteer services, some larger programs employ a volunteer coordinator. The coordinator's job may be to help recruit and screen volunteers, to assess individual staff needs and interests for volunteer assistance, to assign volunteers to suitable activities, and to provide them with training and orientation.

One of the strongest precautions to be taken in the use of volunteers is to ensure that they are never utilized to provide basic program coverage. An agency should always have adequate regular paid staff for this. When programs have counted on a "patchwork" of volunteers to sustain daily activity, the results have sometimes been disastrous. Some volunteers came in late, if they came at all. Others had not had the experience to handle the inevitable crisis situations which developed. It jeopardizes a program and is insulting to volunteers, as well, to place them in positions of ongoing direct responsibility. An exception, perhaps, is a most grave emergency unless the volunteers have the backup presence of regular staff.

Recent programming trends in the use of volunteers have involved using people representing a wide age range. This is done in order to expose the children to a variety of people. High school students and elderly people have been used successfully in this way.

SUMMARY

Effective relationships with the community provide child care programs with essential resources. Professionals in the community may give consulation, help in training potential workers with children, and take part in mutual referral systems.

The general community is the source of consumers of a program. It is also the source of additional resources which support it. A new program is most likely to be successful if the need for it has been assessed and if community leaders have been involved in its planning. Specific kinds of support for programs include funds given through donations or foundations, donations of materials and equipment, and volunteers. Appropriately trained and utilized, volunteers can give greater dimension to a program.

SUGGESTED ACTIVITIES

- Talk to the director of a program which has used a consultant. What were the functions of the consultant? How did the staff react to his suggestions?

- Visit a child care program which also serves as a training site for a local educational program. How are students used in the program? What benefits are gained through their presence? What are some of the problems they have encountered with the students?

- Try to find a child care program in your community which has recently opened. Ask the director or administrator to describe to you the steps taken to develop and establish the program.

- See if you can obtain a copy of the annual report of a foundation. What kinds of programs has it previously funded?. Can you think of a type of program which might be of interest to that foundation for potential funding, based on your knowledge of other types of programs it has supported?

- Visit an agency with a well-established volunteer program. How are the volunteers recruited and prepared for their work? What functions do they perform?

REVIEW

A. Define each of the following.

    1. Consultation   3. Proposal

    2. Foundation   4. Needs assessment

B. Indicate the best choice for each of the following.

    1. A factor contributing towards effective consultation is

        a. Clearly informing staff as to the consultant's role.
        b. Paying the consultant a large fee.
        c. A direct and critical approach by the consultant.
        d. None of the above.

    2. Foundations

        a. Usually supply ongoing funding.
        b. Expect that funds will be used to meet objectives stated in the proposal.
        c. Are the only source of external funding for child care programs.
        d. All of the above.

C. Briefly answer each of the following.

    1. List and define three kinds of consultation in early childhood programs.

    2. Cite two advantages to a program serving as a training site for students.

    3. Describe several ways in which the community provides supportive resources to a program.

    4. List three guidelines which contribute to the effective utilization of volunteers.

unit 15 political factors

OBJECTIVES

After studying this unit, the student should be able to

- Discuss the relationship between child care services and political factors.
- Describe key leglisation related to providing child care services.
- Define the term *accountability* and discuss its relationship to objective setting and evaluation.
- Describe problems associated with the evaluation of child care services.
- Discuss the relationships between licensing, certification, and quality child care.
- Describe the opportunities for professional development available to the child care assistant.
- Define the Child Advocacy Movement.

Not too many years ago, the major focus of persons working with children was on the events that took place in the settings in which they worked. They knew that they were operating with insufficient money to buy proper equipment. They were aware that perhaps next year there would be no money to pay their salaries — which meant that the children they were committed to serve would soon be left without a program. However, they usually accepted these facts as a necessary condition of their work.

Societal changes in more recent years, as described in previous units, have not only restructured the pattern of child rearing practices, but also have changed the attitudes of parents, teachers, child care assistants, professionals, and others who are concerned with children's welfare. No longer do many of these people accept such constraints upon both themselves and the families and children to whom they are committed. There is growing realization that meeting the needs of children means influencing those factors which affect the basic structure of society itself.

Increasing attention is, therefore, being given to the national political scene. Here, major legislative decisions concerning guidelines and funding for human services — which, of course, include early childhood programs — are made. Child care practitioners now recognize that they must make their voices heard at these highest levels of policy making.

This final unit describes some of the ways in which political activity is related to improving child care today. It also covers ways in which the child care assistant can increase his or her effectiveness in working to promote the welfare of children.

LEGISLATION AND GOVERNMENT FUNDING

Many child care programs have had to rely at least partially on outside sources of financial support. Since fees collected from consumers are usually insufficient to cover costs of conducting the program (particularly if they are set according to a sliding scale based on total family income), additional money is required. The preceding unit described private sources of such support, such as foundations and citizen donations.

A major source of external funding, particularly since the inception of the War on Poverty in the early 1960s, has been the federal government. For example, the underwriting of the extensive Head Start Program was provided by federal legislation: The Economic Opportunity Act of 1964. Later on in the 1960s, Congress began to provide subsidy for day care programs as a result of growing recognition of the needs of working mothers for substitute child care. Title IV A and Title IV B of the Social Security Act were amendments made to allocate the needed funds.

Without federal financing, which has totaled millions of dollars, many programs giving essential services would not be in existence at all. However, the provision of governmental support for human services is a highly complex matter.

There has been a lack of agreement among legislators as to the value which is achieved through such programs. Some feel that day care will "break up the family," rather than hold them together by giving them essential supports. Others back the concept of day care, but only for those who would otherwise be on welfare, so that the mothers can go out to work. Still others contend that day care should be for all who feel the need for it and that it should not be used to force mothers who would prefer to stay home into the employment market. Another related point of view is that all mothers should be given a subsidy so that they can stay home. This is based on the assumption that home care is better for children than group programs. Finally, there is debate about the purpose of day care. Should day care be oriented primarily towards providing educational experiences at a time that is important for learning, or should it offer a complete range of health, social, and psychological services as well?

Many are coming to recognize the significance of the early years in children's development. The feminist movement and other groups whose goals include the securing of opportunity for their children are having increased impact. These factors are among those which keep child care programs at the forefront politically. Early in 1975, Title XX – Social Services, was passed as an amendment to the Social Security Act. The Child and Family Services Act of 1975 was also introduced into Congress by Senators Mondale and Brademas, who have previously sponsored child care legislation. This bill proposed a spectrum of comprehensive child care services, subsidized by a suggested allocation of $1.85 billion. The trend towards federal provision of a broad network of family supports is increasing.

ACCOUNTABILITY, OBJECTIVES, AND EVALUATION

As a result of a tight economy, agencies providing subsidy for human services programs have increasingly required that the programs demonstrate *accountability*. Accountability refers to specific accomplishments which justify the expenditure of the funds which was made for them. To show such results, programs must have ways of measuring their effectiveness — of evaluating them. Unfortunately, social service fields in general have failed to develop methods of establishing specific goals for their programs, of designing activities which would lead toward their achievement, and utilizing appropriate methods to determine if the goals were met.

Lack of solid evaluative data on child care programs can have and has had (recall the example of Head Start evaluation described earlier) negative effects. Politicians and legislators base their decisions on concrete evidence. Therefore, they look to evaluative studies to help them decide which programs are the most effective and should be supported. When there is no information on the evaluation of a program, or when what has been gathered is inaccurate or misleading, a decision may be made against a program which actually has merit.

For these reasons, intensive scrutiny is being given today by program planners to the use of more sophisticated and valid evaluation techniques. It is also being given to the use of managerial strategies adapted from the business world which might help them develop strong programs and use available resources effectively. Earlier, it may have been felt that such "hard nosed" methods were counter to the philosophy of human services. Now, it is acknowledged that such prudent and efficient administration is necessary if the programs are to continue to be able to exist.

One well-known managerial technique which is increasingly finding its way into human service programs is *management by objectives*. This involves stating the goals or broader purposes of a program in terms of specific objectives, or end products, to be achieved. From these, specific activities are planned which will meet the objectives.

It is stressed that objectives must be stated in measurable terms. Thus, they need to be precise, rather than general. For example, a program objective which states, "The children will understand the world around them" is a broad and vague statement. "The children will identify the jobs performed by adults in a series of ten pictures," is specific and, therefore, measurable. How can it really be determined to what degree children understand the world around them? It is possible, however, to measure the children's knowledge of adult job functions through their ability to identify them in pictures.

The value of such objectives is that they imply evaluation techniques which are more likely to assure that the achievement of the objective is actually measured. When objectives are not clearly stated, then it is obviously difficult, if not impossible, to determine whether or not they have been achieved.

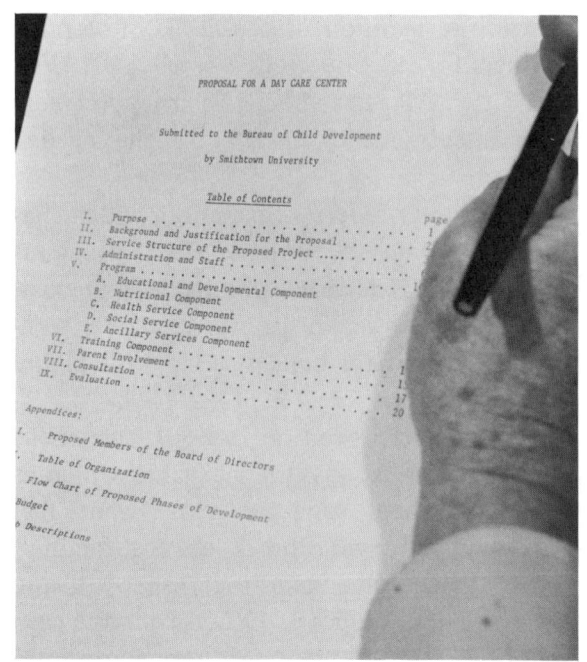

A growing trend in direct programming for children is to describe program goals in terms of *behavioral objectives*. That is, statements will be made in terms of behaviors which can actually be observed following a designated experience. Evidence can be seen that the experience has indeed developed the knowledge or skill it was intended to. The conditions under which such objectives are to be achieved are sometimes stated: "Given cards with five different colors, the child will name four of the colors." Curricular objectives are usually stated in two forms. One is a *cognitive objective* — relating to knowledge and intellect. The other is an *affective objective* — relating to feelings and attitudes.

In terms of helping program and curriculum planners to truly state the goals they wish children in their program to sustain, in a way which can be measured, behavioral objectives are a valuable tool. They are frequently looked upon favorably by those in decision making positions concerning allocation of program support, because they can provide "hard data" regarding a program's accomplishments.

On the other hand, they have been the subject of considerable controversy. Some feel that the constraint of structuring all activities to meet specific objectives has pitfalls. It can detract from the flexibility which is so important for programs serving children. Such qualities as creativity may not be evaluated. Competition may be set up among both children and staff as they race to meet prescribed objectives by a certain time.

There are many issues still to be resolved in the area of accountability, objective setting, and evaluation. Since these concepts are so crucial to today's provision of child care services, it is important that the child care assistant be familiar with them and their implications.

LICENSING AND CERTIFICATION

Making programs accountable to the wider community through evaluation of preestablished objectives is one means of assuring quality control — of assuring that a meaningful and sound program is being conducted. Another mode of quality control is provided through licensing and certification.

Licensing, in the context of child care programming, is the process of evaluating a center to determine whether it conforms to preestablished guidelines. Such guidelines are usually set up and enforced by an external governmental agency. Their purpose is to ensure that the services provided are not harmful to the clients using them. Similar regulations are established by appropriate agencies for a variety of other community services, such as restaurants and beauty parlors, as a means of standards control.

Licensing regulations are applied to various aspects of child care programs. These include ratios of staff to children; factors related to safety of the physical setting, such as space and sanitary facilities; requirements for furnishings and equipment; preparation and training of staff; size of groups; types of services which should be provided; and others.

Licensing regulations have both advantages and disadvantages. On the positive side, they contribute towards the elimination of programs which are truly harmful and damaging. Such programs simply do not get a license. If they are already operational, their licenses are revoked. Without licensure, their continuation is illegal.

Sometimes, licensing regulations are too regid along certain dimensions. This means that otherwise high quality programs which cannot meet a certain requirement are eliminated. For example, a program may have an excellent staff and fine equipment, but not be able to provide a physical setting which can offer each child a specified amount of space. Conversely, some poor programs have continued because the regulations made provision for a bare minimum of essentials or regulated factors which were not the most important in terms of best meeting the needs of the children enrolled. In addition, some regulations are stated in such a way that program operators are able to "get around" them.

One factor contributing to the effectiveness of licensing regulations includes the characteristics of the persons who inspect programs to determine their conformance to the regulations. When there are enough well prepared inspectors able to visit programs frequently and study them carefully, the benfits are naturally positive. Unfortunately, the funding constraints which have affected all human service programs have also had an influence on the provision of a sufficient number of trained persons for this important job.

Certification is a process whereby individual practitioners of a profession are examined by an external body — usually, as in the case of operating programs, a governmental agency — to determine whether they have adequate knowledge and skills necessary to perform the services subsumed under the title of the profession for which they have prepared. For example, teachers must be certified in order to keep positions in the public school system. To be certified, prospective teachers are usually recommended for certification by the educational program in which they trained, after they meet the course requirements and have satisfactory student teaching experience. Many, but not all, early childhood programs require their teachers to be certified. Those that do are generally those which are funded by public agencies.

Like licensure of programs, certification has both advantages and disadvantages. Sometimes certification requirements shut otherwise highly qualified and talented people out of positions in which they could perform credibly, even if they do not meet the formal requirements. Certification does indicate, however, that a person possesses specific recognized skills related to the functions of a certain job. Thus, an agency, when hiring a new staff member, knows exactly what background skills it can expect the person to contribute.

PROFESSIONAL DEVELOPMENT

Opportunity for professional development of those who have chosen careers in child care is another means of upgrading the quality of programs which serve children. Many child care assistants justifiably aspire to higher level positions where they can have greater responsibility and hence a greater impact. The main avenue to such positions are activities which contribute to the practitioner's professional development. Professional development may be achieved through both formal and informal means.

Formal Professional Development

Formal professional development is achieved through participation in educational programs specifically designed to prepare workers with children. There are numerous programs all over the country which offer curricula in child caring professions. Many of these are programs in early childhood education or early child development. Others offer a more general coverage which includes instruction and practical work with children of all ages, both normal and exceptional. There are several recent advances in educational programming which should contribute to professionalization of workers with children.

One of these is the *Career Ladder* concept, which developed out of the social activism of the 1960s. Its purpose is to give people previously denied access to the educational mainstream the opportunity to move into gratifying and adequately paying careers. A career ladder involves the creation or definition of a hierarchy of job functions and the educational levels necessary to perform the job. This makes it possible for persons to have an opportunity to either move sideways into a position similar to the one they already hold or to move upwards by entering the educational program providing the training necessary to perform the next level job. A typical educational career ladder in a field might consist of associate, baccalaureate, and masters' degree programs. The content at each level would become increasingly complex and require the mastery of new skills. The completion of each level qualifies the person to assume a more responsible and demanding job. Career ladders now exist in many human service fields, such as social work, education, and child development.

Competency Based Training

Competency based training is another important development in educating persons to work with children. It is designed to provide the specific skills or competencies necessary to fulfill a job function. In the field of child development, the new Child Development Associate[1] program, established by the Office of Child Development in 1970, is a competency based program. It is designed to provide the staff that is essential for quality child care to be delivered. The Child Development Associate (CDA) is to be a person who, through training or experience, can demonstrate the skills required for effective work with young children. Determination of the possession of these competencies is not to be made on the basis of numbers of courses taken or academic credits earned. Rather, it will be determined by the person's being able to actually show that he or she possesses these particular skills.

The Child Development Associate program offers a means of assessing competencies. It also awards a credential which indicates that the individual thus possesses the body of skills recognized as those subsumed under the title Child Development Associate.

The rationale of the CDA program reflects the current stress on objectives and evaluation, as described in an earlier section of this unit. The receipt of the credential is based upon the candidate's actually demonstrating, in a way which can be measured, the required skills.

While there is a large and apparently growing number of programs which educate workers with children, there is some lack of consistency among them in terms of curriculum structure, role of field work, administrative home, and similar concerns.

As such programs become increasingly coordinated, recognition of the contributions that graduates can make should contribute to the upgrading of care provided for children. As is frequently stated, all the fancy classroom equipment or curriculum materials in the world cannot compensate for staff who are not well prepared in the variety of skills necessary to meaningfully interact with, and program for, young children.

Informal Professional Development

There are several ways in which child care assistants can increase their professional

[1] Jenny W. Klein. "Towards Competency in Child Care." *Educational Leadership*, October, 1973.

competence. These are different from formal educational programs.

Many agencies conduct in-house training programs designed to both develop and upgrade skills necessary to do the job. These efforts are called preservice and inservice training. Carefully planned and substantive training programs can be greatly effective. Such programs can help workers increase their competency in their particular job with the agency and, also, can introduce them to new skills and knowledge which may be transferrable to other positions.

Professional organizations composed of members of a professional discipline who share similar interests and concerns are a major means of advancing both personal professional development and that of the field as a whole. There is a growing number of professional organizations devoted to interests related to children and child care. The National Association for the Education of Young Children is a well-known organization for those concerned with improving care of young children. Associations of Child Care Workers, whose members work directly with children primarily in residential treatment centers but increasingly in day care and other child care models, provide another means of professional interaction. The American Orthopsychiatric Association is an interdisciplinary group whose main concern is the mental health of both children and adults. In recent years, it has given particular attention to the needs of young children in a changing society and the structuring of programs to best serve them.

Membership in, or participation in the activities of, professional organizations offers many benefits. Most hold annual conferences at which those attending can learn about new developments and talk about mutual interests with colleagues. In addition, most professional organizations publish journals and newsletters which also keep members informed of important activities in the field. Many organizations have various categories of membership, so that students who might not be able to afford the full membership fee may still be able to join.

Participation in the activities of professional organizations provides the sense of colleagueship and professional identity which is so essential for practitioners in any field. It establishes a collective voice for speaking on behalf of the children whose welfare the members are committed to promote. Many professional organizations convey their positions to legislative and policy making bodies. They also communicate with academic training programs and encourage an important interchange between education and direct line practice.

CHILD ADVOCACY

One of the greatest signs of the growing importance of the relationship between child care services and the political world is the *child advocacy* movement. Child advocacy is defined as "intervention on behalf of children in relation to those services and institutions that impinge on their lives."[2] This movement, oriented towards actively asserting the necessity to meet the many needs of children, gained impetus during the late 1960s along with other similar movements directed towards the improvement of society.

There are several ways in which child advocacy is carried out. It may involve intervening in legal proceedings affecting children, working to obtain essential services, lobbying for the development and passage of child- and family-centered legislation, and other means.

Advocates may be individual parents whose children are deprived of important services. Through their efforts to secure the services the parents may become advocates for other children in similar circumstances. Professional organizations, as mentioned earlier, may advocate for children's rights, along with many other citizens and professional groups which represent a particular interest or concern.

Specific advocacy groups include The Children's Defense Fund of Cambridge, Massachusetts and the Children's Lobby, which is operational in several states. Groups advocating improvement of child care for their constituencies include the National Organization for Women, which has an active component working for the development of quality child care services, and the Black Child Development Institute of Washington, D.C., which is oriented towards providing child care programming which meets the needs of black children.

THE CHALLENGE OF CHILD CARE

In 1970, the Report of the Joint Commission on Mental Health of Children, *Crisis in Child Mental Health: Challenge for the 1970s,*[3] appeared. This highly significant book, which should be read by every person concerned with the well-being and positive development of children, underscored incisively the tremendous needs of children today for essential services which society must provide.

The child care assistant or teacher who is committed to children, to the profession, and to on-going personal and professional growth, is making a contribution to the effort to give maximum opportunity for healthy growth to today's youth.

SUMMARY

Today, improving the lives of children involves an understanding of the political context in which the quality and nature of child care services is determined. The federal government presently supplies funding to many early childhood programs. Differences among legislators as to the form such programs should take has sometimes impeded the passage of legislation.

Economic factors contribute to a growing trend in which programs must be accountable to their funding agencies. They must show concrete and demonstrable achievements. Objective setting and evaluation are activities important to accountability.

Other modes for achieving quality in programming are licensing of programs and certification of staff. Both have advantages and disadvantages.

Child care assistants may increase their own scope through such activities as further education and participation in professional organizations. The growing child advocacy movement is oriented towards actively seeking those services which children need. The committed child care assistant is a member of a highly challenging field: that of promoting the positive development of children today.

---

[2] A. Kahn, S. Kamerman, and B. McGowan. *Child Advocacy: Report of a National Baseline Study.* Children's Bureau, Office of Child Development, U.S. Department of Health, Education, and Welfare.

[3] New York: Harper and Row, 1969.

Section 6 Community Relationships

SUGGESTED ACTIVITIES

- Arrange to speak with a legislator, such as one of your state senators, if possible. What are his/her opinions about early child care and about curent child care legislation?

- Obtain a copy of the text of a recent piece of child care legislation. Do you feel it is adequate to meet the needs of children?

- Visit a child care agency, and meet with the director. Ask her/him to describe to you the goals and objectives of the program and the means used to evaluate their accomplishment. In your opinion, does the program have an adequately stated component of objectives and of evaluative tools?

- Obtain a copy of the licensing regulations for child care programs in your region or state. Do you think they are adequate to assure quality programming? Are they very rigid or are they only minimal?

- Attend a meeting of a professional organization in your community which is oriented to children and their needs. In what way did your participation in this meeting increase your knowledge of the field and the role you might play in it?

- Secure catalogues from a nearby college or university which offers baccalaureate and/or graduate study in a child-related profession. Do graduates of associate degree programs enroll in these programs? What kinds of positions do you think might be open to graduates? How does the curriculum compare with that of your program?

- Attend a meeting of an advocacy group. What do they specifically want to achieve? What methods are they using to gain the changes they feel are necessary?

REVIEW

A. Define each of the following.
   1. Competency-based training
   2. Child advocacy
   3. Accountability
   4. Licensing

B. Indicate the best choice for each of the following.
   1. The Child Development Associate credential
      a. Is awarded on completion of a certain number of academic credits.
      b. Was established by the Office of Social Welfare.
      c. Is awarded on the basis of demonstrated competencies.
      d. Is equivalent to a college diploma.

2. Legislators
   a. Generally agree on the goals of child care programs.
   b. Often disagree on the goals of child care programs.
   c. Avoid examining evaluative data.
   d. Generally feel day care should be universally available.

3. The most recently proposed child care legislation is
   a. The Economic Opportunity Act.
   b. The Comprehensive Child Development Bill.
   c. The Economic Opportunity Amendments.
   d. The Child and Family Services Act.

4. Which of the following is not a well written behavioral objective?
   a. The child will describe three different animals.
   b. The child will name three colors.
   c. The child will understand two stories.
   d. The child will recognize two shapes.

5. An educational program which offers differing levels of training corresponding to positions in the job market represents a
   a. Child Development Associate Program.
   b. Career Ladder.
   c. Certified Early Childhood Program.
   d. Spiral Curriculum.

6. A professional organization which specifically includes workers in residential centers for children is
   a. National Association for the Education of Young Children.
   b. Society for Research in Child Development.
   c. Association of Child Care Workers.
   d. Association for Childhood Education International.

C. Briefly answer each of the following.
   1. Describe three issues in child care programming which have been of concern to legislators.
   2. Describe the significance of evaluation in child care programs.
   3. Describe both the advantages and disadvantages of licensing and certification.

ANSWERS TO REVIEW QUESTIONS

Unit 1 Factors Influencing Child Development

B. 1. c   4. c   7. c   9. d
    2. c   5. d   8. c   10. c
    3. b   6. b

Unit 2 Cultural Influences on Child Rearing Practices

B. 1. c   6. c
    2. c   7. d
    3. a   8. d
    4. c   9. a
    5. b

Unit 3 The Concept of Early Intervention

B. 1. b   7. c
    2. d   8. b
    3. b   9. c
    4. c   10. a
    5. b   11. d
    6. c

Unit 4 Models of Early Intervention Programs

D. 1. c   5. a
    2. d   6. c
    3. c   7. b
    4. c

Unit 5 Child Care and the Changing Society

D. 1. d
    2. d
    3. b

Unit 6 Special Aspects of Contemporary Child Rearing

B. 1. d   4. a
    2. b   5. a
    3. c   6. c

Unit 7 Models of Substitute Child Care

C. 1. a   4. a
    2. b   5. c
    3. c

Unit 8 Establishing Parent-Teacher Contacts

A. 1. c
    2. a

Answers to Review

Unit 9 Parent Involvement

B.
1. d
2. b
3. c
4. a
5. b
6. d
7. c

Unit 10 Parent Education

B.
1. b
2. c
3. b
4. a
5. b
6. d
7. c
8. c

Unit 11 Working With Parents and Children in the Home

B.
1. b
2. c
3. b
4. c
5. b
6. b

Unit 12 Identifying the Exceptional Child

B.
1. b
2. c
3. c
4. d

Unit 13 The Exceptional Child in Class and Community

B.
1. a
2. c

Unit 14 Program Resources and the Community

B.
1. a
2. b

Unit 15 Political Factors in Contemporary Child Care

B.
1. c
2. b
3. d
4. c
5. b
6. c

BIBLIOGRAPHY

Ainsworth, M.S. "Patterns of Attachment Behavior Shown by the Infant in Interactions with his Mother." In Rebelsky, F., and Dorman, L., eds. *Child Development and Behavior.* New York: Alfred A. Knopf, 1970.

Alternatives in Quality Child Care. Washington, D.C.: Day Care and Child Development Council of America, 1972.

Anderson, R. and Shane, H.G. *As the Twig is Bent: Readings in Early Childhood Education.* Boston: Houghton Mifflin, 1971.

Anderson, S.B. "Educational Compensation and Evaluation: A Critique." In Stanley, J., ed. *Compensatory Education for Children, Ages 2 to 8.* Baltimore: The Johns Hopkins University Press, 1973, 196-207.

Aries, P. *Centuries of Childhood.* New York: Random House, 1962.

Auerbach, A. *Parents Learn Through Discussion: Principles and Practices of Parent Group Education.* New York: John Wiley, 1968.

Auerbach, A. "Trends and Techniques in Parent Education: A Critical Review." New York: Child Study Association of America, 1960.

Axline, V. *Dibs: In Search of Self.* New York: Ballantine Books, 1964.

Becker, W. *Parents are Teachers.* Champaign, Ill.: Research Press, 1971.

Bettelheim, B. *The Children of the Dream.* New York: The MacMillan Company, 1969.

Biller, H. *Father, Child and Sex Role: Paternal Determinants of Personality Development.* Lexington, Mass: D.C. Heath, 1971.

Birch, H.G., and Gussow, J. *Disadvantaged Children: Health, Nutrition, and School Failure.* New York: Grune and Stratton, 1970.

Bowlby, J. *Attachment and Loss. Vol. 1: Attachment.* New York: Basic Books, 1969.

Bowlby, J. *Child Care and the Growth of Love.,* 2d. ed. Baltimore: Penguin Books, 1966.

Boguslawski, D. *Guide for Establishing and Operating Day Care Centers for Young Children.* New York: Child Welfare League of America, 1966.

Brady, E., Deutsch, D., Farr, K., and Gold, B. "The Use of Videotapes in Parent Conferences." *Young Children,* May, 1968, 276-280.

Breitbart, V. *The Day Care Book: The Why, What and How of Community Day Care.* New York: Alfred A. Knopf, 1974.

Brim, O. *Education for Child Rearing.* New York: Free Press, 1965.

Brocher, T. "Parents Schools." *Psychiatric Communications,* Western Psychiatric Institute and Clinic, University of Pittsburgh, Pittsburgh, PA 13(2), 1971.

Bromberg, S. "A Beginning Teacher Works with Parents." *Young Children,* 14(2), December, 1968.

Brown, L. *This Stranger, My Son.* New York: G.P. Putnam, 1968.

Buchanan, R., and Mullins, J. "Integration of a Spina Bifida Child in a Kindergarten for Normal Children." *Young Children,* 13(6), September, 1968.

Burns, L., Childs, L., and Clark, E. "Parents Have Much to Give." *Young Children,* 23(2), November, 1967.

Caldwell, B., and Elardo, R. "Value Imposition in Early Education: Fact or Fancy." *Child Care Quarterly,* 2(1), Spring, 1973.

Bibliography

Caplan, G. "Types of Mental Health Consultation." *American Journal of Orthopsychiatry,* 1963, 33, 470-481.

Champagne, D.W., and Goldman, R.M. *Teaching Parents Teaching.* New York: Appleton-Century Crofts, 1972.

Chess, S., Thomas, A., and Birch, H. *Your Child is a Person: A Psychological Approach to Parenthood Without Guilt.* New York: Parallax, 1965.

Children's Defense Fund: "An Interview With Marian Wright Edelman." *Young Children,* 28(5), June, 1973.

Children Today, (Child Abuse Issue), May-June, 1975, 4(3).

Child study Association of America. *When Parents Get Together: How to Organize a Parent Education Program.* New York: Child Study Association of America, 1964.

Clinebell, C.H. and Clinebell, H.J. *Crisis and Growth: Helping Your Troubled Child,* Philadelphia: Fortress Press, 1971.

Cohen, D.J., in collaboration with A.S. Brandegee. *Day Care 3-Serving Preschool Children.* U.S. Department of H.E. W. Office of Human Development, Office of Child Development, 1974.

Cohen, S. "Integrating Children With Handicaps Into Early Childhood Education Programs." *Children Today,* 4(1), Jan-Feb. 1975.

Curry, N.E. *Current Issues in Play: Theoretical and Practical Considerations for Its Use as a Curricular Tool in the Preschool.* University of Pittsburgh: Division of Instructional Experimentation, 1972.

Curry, L, and Rood, L. *Head Start Handbook for Parents.* Washington, D.C.: Gryphon House, 1975.

Delano, J. "Ten O'Clock Scholars." *Young Children,* 13(1), October, 1967.

Denenberg, V., ed. *Education of the Infant and Young Child.* Academic Press, 1970.

Dittmann, L., ed. *Early Child Care: The New Perspectives.* New York: Athernon Press, 1969.

Dreiss, J. "The Psychological Effects of Fathering on the Child, or What are Daddies For?", *Pittsburgh Area Preschool Association Publication,* 7(4), April, 1974.

Dullea, G. "The Increasing Single Parent Families. . ." *New York Times,* December 3, 1974.

Eiduson, B. "Looking at Children in Emergent Family Styles." *Children Today,* 3(4), July-Aug., 1974, 2-6.

Eisenberg, L. "Strengths of the Inner City Child." In Passow, et. al., eds. *Education of the Disadvantaged: A Book of Readings.* New York: Holt, Rinehart and Winston, 78-87.

Erikson, E.H. *Childhood and Society.* New York: Norton, 1951.

Evans, E.B., Shub, B., and Weinstein, M. *Day Care.* Boston: Beacon Press, 1971.

Evans, E.B., and Saia, G. *Day Care for Infants.* Boston: Beacon Press, 1972.

Friedan, B. *The Feminine Mystique.* New York: Dell Publishing Company, 1963.

Frank, M., ed. *Pittsburgh Area Preschool Association Publication.* "Theme: Adoption" 8(1), October, 1974.

Frank, M., ed. "Theme: Divorce and the Young Child." *Pittsburgh Area Preschool Association Publication* 7(2), November, 1973.

Frank, M., ed. "Theme: Young Children: Political Issues and Public Policy." *Pittsburgh Area Preschool Association Publication* 9(1), November, 1975.

Frank, M., ed. "Theme: The Right to Education." *Pittsburgh Area Preschool Association Publication,* 7(3), February, 1974.

Golden, D., and Davis, J. "Counseling Parents After the Birth of an Infant with Down's Syndrome." *Children Today,* 3(2), March-April, 1974, 7-11.

Goldstein, J., Freud, A., and Solnit, A. *Beyond the Best Interests of the Child.* New York: The Free Press, 1973.

Bibliography

Goller, G. "Use of the Small Discussion Group in Parent Education." *Scoial Work,* April, 1957.

Gordon, I. "Stimulation Via Parent Education." *Children,* 16(2), March-April, 1969, 57-59.

Gordon, T. *Parent Effectiveness Training.* New York: Peter Wyden, 1970.

Grotberg, E., ed. *Day Care: Resources for Decisions.* Office of Economic Opportunity, Office of Planning, Research, and Evaluation, 1971.

Gotkin, L.G. "The Telephone Call: The Direct Line From Teacher to Family." *Young Children,* December, 1968, 270-274.

Harlow, H. "The Nature of Love." in Rebelsky, F., and Dorman, L., eds. *Child Development and Behavior,* New York, Alfred A. Knopf, 1970, 73-88.

Hart, V. "Theme Report." (Right to Education), *Pittsburgh Area Preschool Association Publication,* 7(3), February, 1974.

Heck, T., Gomez, A., and Adams, G. *A Guide to Mental Health Services,* Pittsburgh: University of Pittsburgh Press, 1973.

Hess, R.D., and Bear, R.M. *Early Education: Current Theory, Research and Action.* Chicago: Aldine, 1968.

Hess, R., Bloch, M., Costello, J., Knowles, R., and Largay, D. "Parent Involvement in Early Education." In Grotberg, E., ed. *Day Care: Resources for Decisions.* Office of Economic Opportunity, Office of Planning, Research and Evaluation.

Hess, R., and Shipman, V. "Early Experience and the Socialization of Cognitive Modes in Children." In Rebelsky, F., and Dorman, L., eds. *Child Development and Behavior,* New York: Alfred Knopf, 1970, 311-326.

Howe, L.K., ed. *The Future of the Family.* New York: Simon and Schuster, 1972.

Hunt, J.McV. "The Psychological Basis for Using Preschool Enrichment as an Antidote for Cultural Deprivation" in Passow, et. al., eds. *Education of the Disadvantaged: A Book of Readings.* New York: Holt, Rinehart and Winston, 1967, 174-213.

Joint Commission on Mental Health of Children. *Crisis in Child Mental Health: Challenge for the 1970's.* New York: Harper and Row, 1970.

Jones, R. "Labels and Stigma in Special Education." *Exceptional Children,* 1972, 38, 553-564.

Jordan, J., and Dailey, R., eds. *Not All Little Wagons are Red-The Exceptional Child's Early Years.* Arlington, Virginia Council for Exceptional Children.

Kahn, A., Kamerman, S., and McGowan, B. *Child Advocacy: Report of a National Baseline Study.* Washington, D.C. Office of Child Development, Children's Bureau, Department of Health, Education, and Welfare.

Kaufman, I.G. "Biological Considerations of Parenthood." in Anthony, E.J., and Benedek, T., eds. *Parenthood: Its Psychology and Psychopathology.* Boston: Little Brown, 1970.

Keyserling, M.D. *Windows on Day Care.* New York: National Council of Jewish Women, 1972.

Keister, M.E. *"The Good Life" for Infants and Toddlers.* Washington, D.C. National Association for the Education of Young Children, 1970.

Kessler, J.W. *Psychopathology of Childhood.* Englewood, N.J.: Prentice-Hall, 1966.

Kiester, D. *Consultation in Day Care.* Institute of Government, University of North Carolina at Chapel Hill, 1969.

Klein, J.W. "Child Development Associates: New Professionals, New Training Strategies." *Children Today,* 2(5), September-October 1973, 2-6.

Klein, J. "Mainstreaming the Preschooler." *Young Children,* 30(5), July, 1975.

Klein, J., and Randolph, L. "Placing Handicapped Children in Head Start Programs." *Children Today,* 3(6), November-December, 1974, 7-10.

Kroth, R. *Communicating With Parents of Exceptional Children.* Denver: Love Publishing Company, 1975.

Levy, D. *Maternal Overprotection.* New York: Columbia University, 1943.

Lorenz, S. *Our Son, Ken.* New York: Dell Publishing Company, 1969.

Lundberg, F. and Farnham, M. *Modern Woman: The Lost Sex.* New York: Harper and Bros., 1947.

McFadden, D., ed. *Early Childhood Development Programs and Services.* Washington, D.C.: National Association for the Education of Young Children, 1972.

Model Programs-Compensatory Education: Mother-Child Home Program, Freeport, New York, Washington, D.C.: Office of Education, U.S. Department of Health, Education and Welfare, 1972.

Moskovitz, S. "Behavioral Objectives: New Ways to Fail Children?" *Young Children,* 28(4), April, 1973.

Newman, S. *Guidelines to Parent-Teacher Cooperation in Early Childhood Education.* Brooklyn: Book Lab, 1971.

O'Keefe, R. "Home Start: Partnership With Parents." *Children Today,* 2(1), January-February, 1973, 12-16.

Packard, V. *Nation of Strangers.* New York: Pocket Books, 1974.

Passow, A.H., Goldberg, M., and Tannenbaum, A., eds. *Education of the Disadvantaged: A Book of Readings.* New York: Holt, Rinehart and Winston, 1967.

Perspectives on Child Care. (reprinted form portions of *Inequality in Education,* #13, December, 1972, published by the Harvard Center for Law and Education.) Washington, D.C.: National Association for the Education of Young Children.

Pieper, A. "Parent and Child Centers-Impetus, Implementation, In-Depth View." *Young Children,* 26(2), December, 1970.

Pines, M. *Revolution in Learning.* New York: Harper and Row, 1966.

Prescott, E., and Jones, E., with Kritchevsky, S. *Day Care as a Child Rearing Environment.* Washington, D.C., National Association for the Education of Young Children, 1972.

Prescott, E., Milich, C., and Jones, E. *The "Politics" of Day Care,* Washington, D.C.: The National Association for the Education of Young Children, 1972.

Provence, S. *Guide for the Care of Infants in Groups.* New York: Child Welfare League of America, 1967.

Rafael, B. "Early Education for Multihandicapped Children." *Children Today,* 2(1), January-February, 1972, 22-26.

Rheingold, H., and Eckerman, C. "The Infant Separates From his Mother." *Science,* 1970, 168, 78-83.

Riessman, F., and Popper, H. *Up From Poverty.* New York: Harper and Row, 1968.

Roby, P. *Child Care-Who Cares?* New York: Basic Books, 1973.

Rosaff, S., Marland, S., and Kruger, W. "Education for Parenthood." *Children Today,* 2(2), March-April, 1973, 3-7.

Rossi, A. "Equality Between the Sexes: An Immodest Proposal," *Daedalus,* Spring, 1964.

Rutter, M. *Maternal Deprivation Reassessed.* Middlesex, England: Penguin Books, 1972.

Schaefer, E. "A Home Tutoring Program." *Children,* 16(2), March-April, 1969, 59-61.

Shaw, C.R. *When Your Child Needs Help.* New York: Barnes and Noble, 1972.

Sidel, R. *Women and Child Care in China.* New York: Hill and Wang, 1972.

Siegel, A.E., and Haas, M.B. "The Working Mother: A Review of Research." *Child Development,* 1963, 34, 513-542.

Bibliography

Sigel, I., Secrist, A., and Forman, G. "III. Psycho-Educational Intervention Beginning at Age Two: Reflections and Outcomes." in Stanley, J., ed. *Compensatory Education for Children, Ages 2 to 8,* Baltimore: The Johns Hopkins University Press, 1973, 25-62.

Smilansky, S. *The Effects of Sociodramatic Play on Disadvantaged Children.* New York: John Wiley, 1968.

Stanley, J., ed. *Compensatory Education for Children, Ages 2 to 8: Recent Studies of Educational Intervention.* Baltimore: The Johns Hopkins University Press, 1973.

Steinfels, M.O. *Who's Minding the Children? The History and Politics of Day Care in America.* New York: Simon and Schuster, 1973.

Stone, L.J., and Church, J. *Childhood and Adolescence, Third Edition.* New York: Random House, 1973.

Streuer, E. "Current Legislative Proposals and Public Policy Questions for Child Care." In Roby, P., ed. *Child Care-Who Cares?* New York: Basic Books, 1973.

Taylor, K.W. *Parents and Children Learn Together.* New York: Teachers College Press, 1967.

VanderVen, K. "Caring for our Children: Programs, Problems, Possibilities." PITT Magazine, Spring, 1973.

VanderVen, K. "Child Care and the Changing Roles of Women." *Pittsburgh Area Preschool Association Publication,* 5(2), December, 1971.

VanderVen, K. "From Raising Kids to Parenting: Current Modalities of Parent Education." *Pittsburgh Area Preschool Association Publication,* 6(2), November, 1972.

VanderVen, K. "Infancy-Research, Early Experience, and Child Care Practices — Some Key Issues." *Pittsburgh Area Preschool Association Publication,* 6(4), April, 1973.

VanderVen, K. "The Corporate Transfer Father, Frequent Mobility, and the Impact on Children and Families." *Pittsburgh Area Preschool Association Publication,* 7(4), April, 1974.

Weikart, D., Rogers, C., and Adcock, C. *The Cognitively Oriented Curriculum.* Washington, D.C.: National Association for the Education of Young Children, 1971.

Wenig, M., and Brown, M.L. "School Efforts + Parent/Teacher Communications = Happy Young Children." *Young Children,* 30(5), July 1975.

Wolfensberger, W. *The Principle of Normalization in Human Services.* Toronto: National Institute on Mental Retardation, 1972.

Zigler, E. "Project Head Start: Success or Failure?" *Children Today,* 2(6), November-December, 1973, 2-7.

Acknowledgments

Grateful acknowledgment is extended to those who contributed towards this book:

Dr. Nancy Curry, Chairman, Department of Child Development and Child Care, School of Health Related Professions, University of Pittsburgh, who provided warm and vital support and encouragement throughout the preparation of this work and reviewed the text on its completion.

Dr. Shirley Atkins, Assistant Professor of Child Development and Child Care, School of Health Related Professions, who reviewed Unit 2, "Cultural Influences on Child Rearing Practices" and utilized it in one of her classes. Appreciation is offered for the valuable suggestions which were made as a result of these activities.

Michael Moody whose artistry and photographic skill with children and adults gives special vitality to the book.

Mark Sussman, who provided helpful consultation on illustration.

The Mecklenburg County Center for Human Development (North Carolina) which permitted use of several photographs for Section 5.

Anita Bedeau, who skillfully typed portions of the original manuscript.

The *Pittsburgh Area Preschool Association Publication* (now *Children in Contemporary Society*) which permitted the reprinting of portions of Unit 11, *Parent Education,* which were adapted from a previous article by the author, "From Raising Kids to Parenting-Current Modalities of Parent Education" appearing in the November, 1972 issue.

The editorial staff of Delmar Publishers, including Elinor Gunnerson and Alan Knofla, who were continuously helpful and patient throughout the book's preparation.

Special acknowledgment is made to Ned VanderVen for his overall support.

Contributions by the Delmar Staff

Director of Publications — Alan N. Knofla

Source Editor — Elinor Gunnerson

Consultant — Jeanne Machado

Reviewer — Deanna J. Radeloff

Director of Manufacturing/Production — Frederick Sharer

Production Specialists — Debbie Monty, Patti Manuli, Sharon Lynch, Betty Michelfelder, Margaret Mutka, Jean LeMorta, Lee St. Onge

Illustrators — Tony Canabush, Michael Kokernak, George Dowse

INDEX

A

Activity level, and basic temperament, 9
Adoption
    change in policies, 54
    definition of, 54
Ainsworth, M.S.
    studies of infant attachment, 3-4
American Orthopsychiatric Association, 134
Association of Child Care Workers, 134
Attention span, and basic temperament, 9
Autism, 108
Autonomy, definition of, 6

B

Baby and Child Care (Spock), 85
Battered child syndrome. *See* Child abuse
Becker, Wesley, 87
Behavior, regressive
    in lower class children, 18
Behaviorism (Watson), 85
Bereiter-Engelmann curriculum model, 40
Bettelheim, Bruno, 53
Beyond the Best Interests of the Child, 55
Birch, H.
    studies on basic temperament, 9
Black Child Development Institute, 135
Blindness, 107
Bloom, Benjamin
    studies on critical learning periods, 29
Brain damage, minimal, 108
Brocher, Dr. Tobias, 87

C

Caldwell, B., 46
Career ladder concept, 133
Caretakers
    primary, 5, 30-31
    role of, 5
CDA. *See* Child Development Associate program
Cerebral palsy, 107
Champagne, David, 87
Change, adaptability to, and basic temperament, 9
Chess, S.
    studies on basic temperament, 9
Child, relationships of
    with members of early childhood center, 1
    with mother, 3-4
Child abuse
    incidence of, 55
    legislation against, 56
    prevention of, 56

Child abuse (continued)
    type of parent involved, 56
Child advocacy movement, 134-135
Child care
    challenge of, 135
    comprehensive, 60
    custodial, 59
    group, 61-62
    role of father, 53-54
Child care, substitute
    advantages of, 48
    comparison with interventive programs, 44-45
    comprehensive, 48
    influence of society, 45-49
        early intervention movement, 45-46
        role of women, 46-49
    key issues in, 59
    models of, 59-65
        baby sitters, 64
        foster home care, 64
        group day care, 62-64
        homemaker service, 64
        for infants and toddlers, 60-62
    primary goal of, 44
    reasons for rejection of, 59-60
    sex-role development in, 48-49
Child care programs
    behavioral objectives, 130
    evaluative studies, 130-131
    and general community, 122-126
        donations, 125
        fund raising, 124-125
        needs assessment, 123
        preliminary relationships, 123
        recruitment, 123-124
        utlilization of resources, 124
        volunteers, 125-126
    management of, 131
    and professional community, 120-122
        consultation, 120-121
        inservice programs, 121
        referral system, 122
        training, 121-122
    quality control
        certification, 132
        licensing, 131-132.
Child care workers
    competency based training, 133
    professional development
        formal, 132-133

146

Child care workers (continued)
  informal, 133-134
Child Development Associate (CDA)
  program, 133
Child rearing
  contemporary, 51-57
  cultural influences on, 13-22
  group
    effects on children, 52
    studies of, 52-53
  influence of societal changes, 51-53
  single parent household, 51-52
    effect on children, 52
    support systems, 52
Child Study Association of America, 85, 86
Children
  failure to thrive, 107-108
  hyperactive, 97, 108
  identification of adults with, 69-70
  learning disabled, 108
  meaning to families
    ambivalent feelings of parents, 15
    during pregnancy, 15
    order of birth, 16
  perceptually-motor handicapped, 108
Children, exceptional, 105-118
  attitudes towards, 108-109
  attitudes towards parents of, 109-110
  categories of, 106-108
    brain damaged, 108
    emotionally disturbed, 108
    mentally retarded, 107-108
    physically handicapped, 107
  in the classroom, 114-116
    integration dynamics, 115-116
  definition of, 105
  enrollment in regular programs, 114
  home vs. institutional care, 113
    effect of custodial care, 113
  identifying criteria, 106
  program models for, 116-118
    community mental health programs, 117
    diagnostic clinics, 117
    parental support systems, 118
    residential centers, 117
    special education, 116
    therapeutic preschool, 116-117
  stigma and labeling of, 113-114
Children of the Dream, The (Bettelheim), 53
Children's Defense Fund, 135
Children's Lobby, 135
Cognitively Oriented Curriculum, The, 40

Collaboration between child caretakers, 69
Communication, parent-teacher, 68-102
  barriers to, 71
  breaking barriers to, 71-73
    contacts, 71-72
    empathizing with parents, 73
    language choice, 72
    respect for parents' opinions, 72-73
  factors influencing, 69-71
    attitudes towards experts, 70-71
    attitudes towards parents, 70
    identification with children, 69-70
  improved by home visits, 98
  interpersonal, 69
  as means of collaboration, 69
  structural, 73-74
    audiovisuals, 74
    parent-teacher meetings, 73
    telephone calls, 73-74
    written forms, 73
Crisis in Child Mental Health: Challenge for the 1970s, 135
Cultural factors
  effect on life-styles, 13
  importance to child care worker, 14
Culture, influence of
  in America, 14
  in pluralistic society, 13-14
Curriculum
  Bereiter-Engelmann model, 40
  cognitive, 39, 45
  Cognitively Oriented Curriculum model, 40
  facilitating, 39
  in Head Start programs, 39-40
  the Montessori method, 40
  play-based, 39-41

D

Day care
  commercial, 64
  comparison with other programs, 62-63
  description of centers, 62
  parent cooperatives, 64
  payment for, 63-64
  staffing of centers, 63
Day care homes
  description of, 60
  drawbacks of, 60-61
  quality control in, 60
Deafness, 107
Deprivation, cultural

Index

Deprivation, cultural (continued)
   criticism of term, 26
   definition of, 26
   experiences lacking in, 26
Deprivation, maternal
   definition of, 4
   in institutions, 4-5
Distractibility, and basic temperament, 9
Down's syndrome, 107

E

Early Child Stumulation Through Parent Education program, 37
Early Education Project for Multihandicapped Children, 116
Early intervention
   age of children receiving, 28
   comparison with substitute child care, 44-45
   concept of, 25-31
   definition of, 27
   essentials of, 30
   evolution of concept, 26-27
      cultural deprivation, 26
      disadvantaged groups, 26
      recognition of cultural differences, 27
   role of federal government, 27
   impact on child care programs, 45-46
   organized stimulation in, 31
   primary goal, 44
   program types
      compensatory, 28
      custodial, 28
      enrichment, 28
      remedial, 28
   rationale of, 28-30
      critical learning periods, 29
      early experience, 28
      environmental quality, 29
      motivation, 29-30
      nutrition, 29
   related concepts
      primary prevention, 27
      secondary prevention, 27-28
      tertiary prevention, 28
   role of parents, , 30-31
   timing, 35
Early intervention, models of, 35-41
   basic forms, 35
   child-centered group models, 38-41
   parent and home-centered models, 35-38
      Education for Parenthood, 35-36
      infants' and toddlers' programs, 37-38

Early Intervention, models of (continued)
      pregnant unmarried mothers' programs, 37
      prenatal and postnatal care, 36-37
Economic class, effects on child rearing practices, 18-19
Economic Opportunity Act (1964), 27, 129
Education
   for parenthood, 35-36
   for pregnant unmarried mothers, 37
   prenatal and postnatal, 36-37
   television, 38
Education for Parenthood
   "parenting," 36
   rationale of, 35
   timing of, 36
"Eight Stages of Man" (Erikson), 2, 6
Eisenberg, L.
   studies on inner city children, 21
Elardo, R., 46
Environment
   influence on developing child, 1, 4, 9
   quality of, 29
Erikson, Erik, 2
Exceptional Parent, The (magazine), 118

F

Family structure, American
   extended
      definition of, 16
      in ethnic groups, 17
   nuclear
      defininition of, 16
      effects of, 16
      emotions in, 16-17
Farnham, M., 47
Father
   absence of, 53
   role in child care, 53-54
      effect of flexible "life-styles," 53
   role in infant development, 8
   and sex-role development, 53-54
Foundations, 124-125
Frank Porter Graham Child Development Center, 38-39

G

Genetics, and child development, 1
Goldman, Richard, 87
Gordon, Dr. Ira, 37
Gordon, Dr. Thomas, 87

H

Harlow experiments, 3-4

Index

Head Start. *See* Project Head Start
Home tutoring program, 37
Home visitation, 95-102
   in early intervention program, 95
   for handicapped children, 96
   infant stimulation programs, 95-96
   maintaining confidentiality in, 101
   problems in, 101
   for program recruitment, 96
   for therapeutic treatment, 96
   value of, 96-98
Home visitors
   activities of, 100-101
   qualities of, 98-100
Homemakers, 64, 101
Hunt, J. McV.
   motivational studies of, 30

I

Individuality
   in psychological development, 8-9
   research studies in, 9
Infant care, 85
Infants
   group care for, 61-62
   interventive programs for, 37-41
   substitute care for, 60-62
Inner city culture
   effects on early learning experiences, 19
   health services in, 20
   individuality in, 21
   language style in, 21
   matriarchal structure of, 20
   play areas in, 19
   racism and, 20
   strengths of, 21
Intervention, early. *See* Early intervention

K

Kaufman, I.G.
   studies in multiple mothering, 8
Keister, Mary Elizabeth, 61
Kessler, J.W.
   study of prevention, 27-28
Kibbutzim, 52-53

L

Learning, critical periods of, 29
Levenstein, Phyllis, 37
Levy, Dr. David, 6
Lost Sex, The (Lundberg and Farnham), 47
Lundberg, F., 47

M

Mainstreaming, 114
Mobility
   corporate, 17
   definition of, 17
   disruptive effects of, 17
Montessori, Dr. Maria, 40
Montessori method, 45
Mood, and basic temperament, 9
Mother-Child Home Program, 37
Mother-child relationship
   attachment, 3-4
   basic trust, 2-3
   temperament, 3
   touching, 3
Mothering
   extremes of, 6
   multiple, 7-8, 52, 61
      definition of, 7
      studies of, 8
Mothers
   family day care, 60-61
   unmarried, programs for, 37
   working, 47-48
Motivation
   competence, 30
   intrinsic, 30
   in learning, 29-30

N

National Association for the Education of Young Children, 134
Normalization, 114
Nutrition
   education, 36
   in interventive programs, 30
   and mental ability, 29

O

Office of Child Development, programs of, 35-36
Office of Education, programs of, 35-36
Overprotection, maternal, 5-6

P

Paraprofessionals, indigenous, 101
Parent-Child Centers, rationale of, 38
Parent cooperatives, 79-80
Parent education, 84-91
   comparison with therapy, 84
   current forms of, 85-88
      experiential model, 87-88
      group education, 86-88

Index

Parent education (continued)
    mass media, 86
    parent corners, 85-86
    parent-teacher conferences, 85
  definition of, 84
  history of, 84-85
  program development and selection, 88-90
    consideration of learning style, 88-89
    cultural considerations, 89
    economic backgrounds, 89
    parent needs, 88
    sequential model, 90
    theoretical vs. practical, 89
  program guidelines, 90-91
    objectives, 90
    physical space, 90
    publicity, 90-91
    resources, 90
    staff selection, 90
  role of assistant teacher in, 91
Parent educators, indigenous, 37
Parent Effectiveness Training Program, 87
Parent involvement, 76-81
  cooperatives, 79-80
  definition of, 76
  dynamics of, 80-81
  effect of societal changes on, 76-77
  forms of, 77-80
    advisory boards, 78
    board of directors, 77-78
    policymaking, 77
  government and, 77
  program participation, 78
  program support, 78-79
    fund raising, 79
  rationale for, 77
Parent-teacher contacts. *See* Communication, parent-teacher
"Parenting," definition of, 36
Parents
  abusive, 55-56
  adoptive, 55
  foster, 54
  psychological, 55
  single, 51-52
"Parents Anonymous," 56
Parents Are Teachers (Becker), 87
Parents Without Partners, 52
Piaget, Jean, 40
Placement
  definition of, 54
  needs in, 55

Placement (continued)
  rights of children, 54
Play, sociodramatic, 40-41
Project Head Start, 27, 38, 76, 85, 96, 129
  curriculum models in, 39-40
  parent support, 39
  purpose of, 39
Psychoses, childhood, 108

R

Regularity, biological, and basic temperament, 9
Reinforcement, positive, 87
Relationship, interpersonal, role in intellectual development, 30
Response intensity, and basic temperament, 9

S

Schaeger, Earl, 37
School
  communication and, 69
  role in child care, 68-69
Sensory deprivation concept, 5
Sensory threshold level, and basic temperament, 9
Separation
  anxiety, 7
  definition of, 7
  detachment process, 7
  effects of, 6
  sequences of, 7
  timing of, 7
Sesame Street, 45
  criticisms of, 38
  purpose of, 38
Sex-role
  development, 48
  stereotyping, 48-49
Skills, cognitive
  in culturally deprived children, 26
Slavson, S.W., 86
Smilansky, Dr. Sara, 40-41
Social Security Act, Title IV-A, IV-B, 27, 129
Society, pluralistic
  definition of, 13
  life-styles in, 13
Spina bifida, 107
Spock, Dr. Benjamin, 85
Stigmatization, 114
Stimulation
  infant, 37
  in infant development, 5
  verbal, 37-38
  verbal interaction materials, 38

Substitute child care. *See* Child care, substitute

T

Teacher-parent contacts. *See* Communication, parent-teacher
Teaching Parents Teaching (Champagne and Goldman), 87
Temperament, basic
   definition of, 8-9
   dimensions of, 9
   reaction to new situations, 9
Their Mother's Sons (Strecker), 47
Thomas, A.
   studies on basic temperament, 9
Toy demonstrators, 38

U

Urban renewal, 19

W

Watson, John, 85
Weikhart, David, 40
White, Robert
   motivational studies of, 30
Wolfensberger, Wolf, 114
Women
   changing roles of, 46-49
      impact on child care, 46-49
      maternal deprivation research, 47
      "momism," 48
      Women's Liberation Movement, 46-48
      working mothers, 48
Wylie, Philip, 47

FUNDERBURG LIBRARY

MANCHESTER COLLEGE